THANK YOU

by

Liggy Webb

**Grosvenor House
Publishing Limited**

This book is published by
Grosvenor House Publishing Ltd
28-30 High Street, Guildford, Surrey, GU1 3EL.
www.grosvenorhousepublishing.co.uk

A CIP record for this book
is available from the British Library

ISBN 978-1-908596-51-2

o

If the only prayer you said in your whole life was "thank you", that would suffice.

Meister Eckhart

Before I close my eyes each night, at the end of every day

There is something very important, that I always like to say

Thank You

Thank you for the things I've learnt, they teach me how to know

Thank you for my challenges, they show me how to grow

Thank you for the good times and thank you for the bad

It helps me to appreciate what I have and haven't had

Thank you for my family and thank you for each friend

You are so very special and all that matters in the end

Thank you for my experiences and thank you for my past

For the magic of the memories through my lifetime that will last

Thank you for my journey and the dreams I'm going to live

Thank you for my future and for the best I've yet to give

So before I close my eyes each night what I really want to say

Is thank you for my life and thank you for today.

© Liggy Webb

This book is dedicated to
Nicholas Anderson
YPX

Contents Page

Introduction

One of the most inspiring conversations that I have experienced occurred whilst I was in Afghanistan working as a consultant with the United Nations in early 2011.

Having been involved with the UN for the last few years, I have been privileged enough to visit various stations and peace missions around the world. Witnessing first-hand some of the amazing work that the organisation and the people within it do is truly life-affirming.

I was especially curious and excited about visiting Afghanistan. Watching the news and hearing so many stories filled me with some trepidation, and as my plane flew down over the breathtakingly beautiful snow-peaked mountains surrounding Kabul, I could feel the tremors of anticipation.

I am not sure that anything could have prepared me for what I was about to encounter, and as my armoured vehicle transported me to my accommodation, I tried to absorb the sights along the way. On arrival at my "guest house", which was heavily guarded and surrounded by barbed wire and sand bags, I was somewhat in awe of the very basic conditions.

Despite the underlying tension, the obvious poverty, the guns, the guards and the grime, the one thing that was most apparent to me was the raw beauty of the country and, most of all, the people. The strength and generosity of spirit was almost palpable. Every moment I stayed in Kabul was an education. Every person I spoke to held a fascinating story and I spent my time enthralled by a cast of extraordinary individuals.

The conversation that resonated with me most of all, however, occurred when I was speaking with one of the delegates in my group. He was a *mullah* – a Muslim man educated in Islamic theology and sacred law. He had been working with the United Nations Office on Drugs and Crime for some years. I shared with him my intention of writing a book about gratitude and we discussed at length the concept of appreciation and happiness. Having been absorbed in research on this subject for many years, I have developed an insatiable curiosity for people's opinions on the subject, so I was eager to hear yet another perspective.

As you can imagine, the situation and circumstances in Afghanistan are incredibly challenging and, from a Western perspective, it can be difficult to comprehend what people would have to be grateful for or happy about.

However, as I shared this somewhat narrow view, I was immediately challenged by the mullah, who looked at me with calm and gentle eyes and said: "Being happy in life isn't so complicated. I have come to appreciate that as long as you have something to love, something to do that gives you a purpose and something to hope for and believe in, then you will always have something to be grateful for." As he smiled at me, I was struck by a glow in his eyes that spoke volumes.

Nothing in my life has humbled me more or made me appreciate the importance of the simplification of our existence.

I returned from Afghanistan a richer person, although certainly not for any material gain. As I returned in transit via Dubai, I pondered the expressions on the people's faces as they roamed the duty free shops greedily clutching bags full of *stuff*. With dull expressions, they were eyeing up designer goodies, perhaps in the hope that some void could be filled that would help them to appreciate their lives more.

I am sure that it suits the consumer bandwagon that we remain in some kind of dissatisfied state so that we are constantly dipping into our pockets and battering our credit cards in the pursuit of happiness and satisfaction.

However, in my humble opinion, I have come to the resounding conclusion that happiness is not *out there*! We seek it here, we seek it there, in fact we seek it everywhere and, all along, it's inside us. If you don't feel it right now, it's because you haven't woken it up. Looking within and appreciating what we have and making the best and most of it is the most empowering ability we possess.

By taking more personal responsibility, we can achieve some amazing things. We are incredible creatures and appreciating ourselves, other people and everything that the world has to offer is an ability that is totally within our control.

We are very fortunate as human beings because we have choice. Certainly, we may not be able to change certain situations and circumstances; however, we can choose how we perceive and process them.

A few months ago, I was presenting at a large conference for a team of sales people. I was speaking about the concept of taking time each day to consider what we are grateful for. I explained how scientific evidence that gratitude improves health comes from research accumulated by Robert Emmons, professor of psychology at the University of California. Dr Emmons, through extensive research, has found that gratitude can make you up to 25% happier.

I introduced the concept of Vitamin G (Vitamin Gratitude - although Vitamin G used to be the old term for Riboflavin, so try not to get confused, even though both are very good for you!) I suggested to everyone that they take a gratitude stone in their hands each morning or evening and just spend a few minutes reflecting on all the things in their lives that they are grateful for. I then offered a range of gratitude stones that I had brought along to everyone in the audience.

A participant on the front row caught my attention when I saw him mouth to the colleague sitting next to him, "What a load of B******t!" Clearly, he wasn't taken with the concept, so I suggested to him that it was his choice to come and take a stone and if he didn't want to, then that was perfectly OK; different things work for different people. Rather begrudgingly, however, he came up and took his stone.

About two weeks later, he telephoned me. He introduced himself and said: "You probably don't remember me." *Oh yes, I do!* I thought.

He explained politely how he had enjoyed my presentation, although that he hadn't really bought into the gratitude concept. He wanted to tell me, however, what had happened to him when he got home. He had lent his brand new car to his wife for the day, and when she had greeted him, somewhat pale-faced and anxious at the front door, she announced that she had two pieces of bad news.

The first piece of news was that she had reversed the car out of the drive and driven too close to the gate and scratched all the paint work along the right-hand door. As he had prepared to rant, she had then dropped the second bombshell, which was that their youngest son had been suspended from his very expensive boarding school. The reason was for his general bad attitude and for not delivering work projects on time consistently. He explained to me that he had been furious, especially considering that he worked ridiculous and gruelling hours to keep his family comfortable.

He had gone upstairs in a very bad mood and as he was getting undressed, he came across his stone. Feeling totally fed up, he had sat on his bed and seriously questioned the concept of gratitude.

He then explained to me that it had been one of the most emphatic moments for him, because two things had occurred to him immediately that he could be grateful for. The first was that his wife had scratched the car and he had suddenly thought: *So what? At least she hasn't been hurt.* The second was that, despite the fact that his son was going through a challenging adolescent phase, at least he wasn't on drugs like some of his friends' children — which was a far worse situation.

He said that he had called me to share this epiphany with me, as he wanted me to know that a daily dose of Vitamin G *does* work and now he keeps his stone on his desk and calls him Rocky!

I really must now credit this man for providing me with a great tale to tell when I talk about gratitude.

My aim with this book is to explore the concept of gratitude and how we can appreciate and enjoy our lives more; how we can use the behaviour and a mindset of gratitude to alleviate stress and depression, develop better relationships with ourselves and others and ultimately improve the quality of our lives. There is some very interesting research now on the subject, with an increasing recognition that people who learn how to appreciate life are happier and healthier. It is also a great way to combat depression, an increasing health concern, with the World Health Organization citing that depression will be the second biggest form of global illness by 2020.

Certainly, I believe that gratitude is a behaviour that can be learned and become a habit! What a great habit, then, to possess!

Imagine waking up every day appreciating your life and appreciating everything and everyone around you. As my father regularly says to my mother when he brings her a cup of coffee in the morning: "Have you woken up with an attitude of gratitude?"

My hope is that this book will inspire you to do just that!

Happy Reading.

CHAPTER ONE

The Benefits of Gratitude

*He is a wise man who does not grieve for the things
which he has not, but rejoices for those which he has.*

Epictetus

I am sure we can all think of times in our lives when
we've expressed heartfelt thanks and realised how
positive it has made us feel. Being grateful has one of the
best feel-good factors and scientific research has
indicated that it can make us happier and healthier too.

Gratitude and being thankful is an almost universal
concept amongst cultures throughout the world. In fact,
nearly all of the world's spiritual traditions emphasise
the importance of giving thanks. Robert Emmons, a
leader in the field of gratitude research at the University
of California has spent the last ten years researching
gratitude. His new book *Thanks: How the New Science
of Gratitude Can Make You Happier* is full of fascinating
reading material, and I highly recommend it.

The key message that Dr Emmons highlights is that the
practise of appreciation can increase happiness levels
by around 25%. He believes that this is not difficult to
achieve and that even a few hours spent writing a

gratitude journal over a three-week period can create an effect that lasts for six months, if not more. The research findings have also indicated that cultivating an attitude of gratitude can bring other health benefits, such as longer and better-quality sleep time.

Feeling grateful has a number of other benefits, too. Feelings of gratitude are associated with less frequent negative emotions and can promote more positive emotions, such as feeling energised, alert, and enthusiastic. You can even experience pleasant muscle relaxation when recalling situations in which you were grateful. It is apparent that the act of giving thanks can have a remarkable impact on a person's well-being, and the best thing is that we can tap into this amazing resource any time we like!

An appreciative mindset can have a very powerful effect on the way we perceive our reality and ultimately, the way we live our lives. By cultivating an attitude of gratitude, we can seek out and attract more positive things into our life to be grateful for.

The film *The Gratitude Experiment,* from the creator of *The Opus*, Douglas Vermeeren, is an interesting film that explores the powerful expanding properties that gratitude possesses in a scientific way. It is certainly very interesting and the studies in this film attempt to demonstrate that gratitude can change negative situations into positive ones in a calculated scientific way.

The important thing about having an attitude of gratitude however is the quality of the feeling that accompanies it.

The study of gratitude within the field of psychology only began around the year 2000, possibly because psychology has traditionally been more focused on understanding distress than understanding positivity. However, with the advent of the Positive Psychology Movement, gratitude has become a mainstream focus of research.

The main conclusions that have been drawn so far are that grateful people report higher levels of positive emotions, life satisfaction, vitality, optimism and lower levels of depression and stress. The disposition toward gratitude appears to enhance the feel-good factor. Grateful people, however, do not deny or ignore the negative aspects of life; they simply focus on the potentially positive outcomes that can be manifested. They seek to turn problems into opportunities and create *probortunities*!

People with a strong disposition toward gratitude have the capacity to be more empathic and find it easier to take the perspective of others. They are rated as more generous and more helpful by people in their social networks.

Grateful people are more likely to acknowledge a belief in the interconnectedness of all life and a commitment to and responsibility for others. Gratitude does not necessarily require religious faith. However, faith and belief in something enhances the ability to appreciate.

It also appears that grateful individuals place less importance on material goods; they are less likely to judge their own and others' success in terms of possessions accumulated; they are less envious of others and are more likely to share their possessions with others.

In a comparative study, those who kept gratitude journals on a weekly basis exercised more regularly, reported fewer negative physical symptoms, felt better about their lives as a whole, and were more optimistic about the upcoming week compared to those who recorded neutral life events.

A related benefit was also observed with regards to personal goal achievement. Participants who kept gratitude lists were more likely to have made progress toward important personal goals over a two-month period compared to subjects under other experimental conditions.

A daily gratitude intervention with young adults resulted in higher reported levels of the positive states of alertness, enthusiasm, determination, attentiveness and energy.

Participants in the daily gratitude condition were also more likely to report having helped someone with a personal problem or having offered emotional support to another person.

Research has also identified that children who practice grateful thinking have more positive attitudes toward school and their families.

Gratitude plays a key role in positive illness management and in a sample of adults with neuromuscular disease, a 21-day gratitude intervention resulted in greater amounts of high energy positive moods, a greater sense of feeling connected to others, more optimism about their lives, and better sleep duration and quality.

Studies also provide evidence that a positive, appreciative attitude enhances the body's healing system and general health by helping your body to produce more immune-boosting endorphins.

When you hold feelings of thankfulness for at least 15 to 20 seconds, beneficial physiological changes take place in your body. Levels of the stress hormones cortisol and norepinephrine decrease, producing a cascade of beneficial metabolic changes. Coronary arteries relax and increase the blood supply to your heart. Your breathing becomes deeper, raising the oxygen level of your tissues.

Gratitude has been the "forgotten factor" in happiness research and scientists are latecomers to the concept of gratitude. Religions and philosophies have long embraced gratitude as an indispensable manifestation of virtue and an integral component of health, wholeness and well-being. Through conducting highly focused studies on the nature of gratitude, its causes, and its consequences, scientists now hope to shed important scientific light on this important concept.

We can only be said to be alive in
those moments when our hearts
are conscious of our treasures.

Thornton Wilder

CHAPTER TWO

What is Gratitude?

Gratitude is not only the greatest of virtues,
but the parent of all the others.

Cicero

Gratitude is about appreciating and being thankful for what you have. The important thing about having an attitude of gratitude is the quality of the feeling that accompanies it.

Living with an attitude of gratitude can mean different things to different people, depending on your background and experiences in life. It can carry with it either good or not-so-good feelings. The kind of gratitude that the self-improvement gurus are recommending is obviously the good-feeling kind. This is the kind that is connected with a positive kind of gratitude attitude.

Living in gratitude with a feeling of indebtedness or subservience to someone is definitely not the kind that supports the growth of happiness. This is emotional imprisonment. It is demeaning and not at all healthy, in my opinion.

This first kind is tinged with fear of loss, feelings of inferiority and a sense of being beholden to someone else for what they have made possible for you. It carries with it the feelings of being a victim in life, and being dependent on others for one's own well-being.

The "good" gratitude is quite different. It has a very positive feeling about it. It is not contrived, but rather a spontaneous bursting forth from inside of a positive energy of real appreciation. It is accompanied by feelings of joy, love and positive energy. If it involves another person, the feeling is often shown physically by a reaching out and wanting to hug them. If it is a feeling of gratitude with no other individual involved, it is still a good feeling, and is usually accompanied by a desire to be thankful anyway. This is where many people direct their thankfulness and gratitude towards life itself or towards an unseen creative power.

The link between spirituality and gratitude has become a popular subject of study in recent years. Research has discovered that spirituality is capable of enhancing a person's ability to be grateful.

Gratitude is viewed as a prized human propensity in the Christian, Buddhist, Muslim, Jewish, and Hindu traditions. Worship is a common theme in religion and therefore, the concept of thankfulness permeates religious texts, teachings, and traditions. For this reason, it is one of the most common emotions that religions aim to provoke and maintain and is regarded as a universal religious sentiment.

In Judaism, gratitude is an essential part of the act of worship and a part of every aspect of a worshipper's life. According to the Hebrew worldview, all things come from God and because of this, gratitude is extremely important to the followers of Judaism. The Hebrew Scriptures are filled with the idea of appreciation.

Gratitude has been said to mould and shape the entire Christian life. Martin Luther King referred to gratitude as "the basic Christian attitude" and today it is still referred to as "the heart of the Gospel". As each Christian believes they were created by God, they are strongly encouraged to praise and give thanks to their creator. Gratitude in Christianity is an acknowledgement of God's generosity that inspires Christians to shape their own thoughts and actions around such ideals. Instead of simply a sentimental feeling, Christian gratitude is regarded as a virtue that shapes not only emotions and thoughts, but also actions and deeds as well.

The Islamic book, the Quran, is filled with the idea of gratitude. Islam encourages its followers to be grateful and express thanks to God in all circumstances. Islamic teaching emphasises the idea that those who are grateful will be rewarded with great pleasures. A traditional Islamic saying states that "the first who will be summoned to paradise are those who have praised God in every circumstance". The Pillar of Islam, calling for daily prayer, encourages believers to pray to God five times a day in order to thank him for his goodness. The pillar of fasting during the month of Ramadan is for the purpose of putting the believer in a state of appreciation.

Gratitude is not just about saying "thank you". It is also about living in a state of thankfulness. It is about truly appreciating the people, experiences and circumstances that create an existence that is unique to you. Gratitude is a state of being which, when cultivated properly, projects itself from an individual out into the world. It is not a reflective force; rather it generates its own source of energy from within. It is the internal combustion engine that powers our desire to help one another. Without gratitude, the seeds of hope and appreciation are never sown, and in their place the weeds of selfishness and self-pity are allowed take root. Gratitude, as the famous Roman orator Cicero said, is the parent of all other virtues. If you're looking for a good place to start improving your life, it would be good to begin by expressing those things for which you are grateful.

So I have a question for you. Do you have an attitude of gratitude? Are you thankful for each and every thing that you have in your life right now, or are you walking around complaining about what you are lacking?

Take full account of the excellencies which you possess, and in gratitude remember how you would hanker after them, if you had them not.

Marcus Aurelius

CHAPTER THREE

The Invisible Patient

*Real life isn't always going to be perfect or go
our way, but the recurring acknowledgement
of what is working in our lives can help us not
only to survive but surmount our difficulties.*

Sarah Ban Breathnach

According to The World Health Organization,
depression will be the second biggest cause of illness
worldwide by 2020. The UK mental health charity
MIND claims that one in four of us will experience a
mental health problem at some point in our lifetimes,
meaning that all of us will be directly affected, either by
experiencing depression ourselves or supporting
someone else who does.

For everyone who suffers, it is different. At its most severe,
depression can be life-threatening, with nearly a million
associated suicides each year worldwide, according to the
latest World Health Organization statistics.

Depression is a serious illness and there is still a huge
stigma attached to it. As it is not an obviously tangible
illness, many people can almost feel like the invisible
patient and are left feeling isolated and desperate in

some situations whilst trying to make sense of what can be a crippling illness.

Health professionals use the words depression, depressive illness or clinical depression to refer to it. It is very different from the common experience of feeling miserable or fed up for a short period of time.

Women are twice as likely to suffer from depression as men, although men are far more likely to commit suicide. This may be because men are more reluctant to seek help for depression.

Gratitude has been said to have one of the strongest links with mental health of any character trait. Numerous studies suggest that grateful people are more likely to have higher levels of happiness and lower levels of stress and depression. In one study concerning gratitude, participants were randomly assigned to one of six therapeutic intervention conditions designed to improve the participant's overall quality of life. Out of these conditions, it was found that the biggest short-term effects came from a "gratitude visit", where participants wrote and delivered a letter of gratitude to someone in their life. This condition showed a rise in happiness scores by 10 percent and a significant fall in depression scores, results which lasted up to one month after the visit.

Out of the six conditions, the longest lasting effects were caused by the act of writing "gratitude journals", where participants were asked to write down three things they were grateful for every day. These participants' happiness scores also increased and continued to increase each time they were tested periodically after the experiment. In fact, the greatest benefits were usually found to occur around six months after treatment began. This exercise was so successful that, although participants were only asked to continue the journal for a week, many continued to do so long after the study was over. Similar results have been found from studies conducted by Dr Emmons, as mentioned before.

Whilst many emotions and personality traits are important to well-being, there is evidence that gratitude may be unique. With this in mind, if you do suffer from depression or know of someone who does, it is well worth trying gratitude exercises, I have found this incredibly effective *especially* during bouts of depression. First thing in the morning is the most recommended time of day, as this very often is the most difficult time of day for people. Waking up with an attitude of gratitude and focusing on the all the things that you are really grateful for is the most positive time to start the day. Using a gratitude stone, as I mentioned in the introduction, is fun, and if you keep it by your bedside or toothbrush you will remember to do this.

Something fun at the end of the day is to do "highlights": summarising the three best things about your day. This is something that can be shared with your family and friends too, as it will encourage others around you to focus on the positive aspects of their day. It's something good to do around the dinner table with children, or phone a friend, or the use the last conversation you have at night with your partner.

The Gratitude Journal at the end of the book helps you to identify your daily highlights and is a great way to summarise the day so that you can fall asleep with a positive attitude and a happier heart.

Gratitude can transform common days into thanksgivings, turn routine jobs into joy, and change ordinary opportunities into blessings.

William Arthur Ward

CHAPTER FOUR

An Attitude of Gratitude

*For there is nothing good or bad,
but thinking makes it so.*

William Shakespeare

Wise words from William! Whether you want to have an attitude of gratitude or not is absolutely up to you. It is your choice. The way that you feel on a day-to-day basis is determined solely by how you think.

On average, we have around 60,000 to 80,000 thoughts a day and this means that the quality of your thoughts is responsible for how you feel and behave. The inner dialogue that goes on in your mind can propel you to embrace and appreciate life or regard it with disappointment and negativity. It's up to you.

True, life is full of challenges: we face disappointment, frustrations, financial problems and a constant battery of impending negativity delivered to us from the daily media doom-goblins.

It also seems to be part of the human condition that we blame others for making us feel a certain way. However, no one can make you feel anything unless you allow them to. The same is true with our life experiences. We will only feel negativity and disappointment if we allow ourselves to feel it. We are totally responsible for how we feel. Our perception is our reality and vice-versa.

So called "realists" can be rather scathing about people with a positive mindset. However, a quote I read in James Borg's rather fabulously-named book *Mindpower* sums it all up rather well:

> *Whether you're an optimist or a pessimist*
> *may not affect the outcome.*
>
> *It's just that the optimist will have*
> *a better time in life!*

I think wise quotes can resonate so powerfully – hence the reason that this book is full of them!

How we cope with everyday challenges and how we focus on the positive outcomes and what there is to appreciate in each situation is purely down to the way we think about it and how we filter it into our world.

Listening to our internal thoughts and challenging and changing the way we think will help us to feel so much better and help us to cultivate an appreciative and positive attitude.

Just over 50 years ago, the clinical psychologist Albert Ellis helped to raise awareness of the importance of changing unhealthy negative thinking with his own

Rational Emotive Behaviour Therapy (REBT), which paved the way for today's highly successful Cognitive Behavioural Therapy (CBT).

We live in such an exciting time where we know so much more about the human brain and subsequently the human mind. Understanding that thinking is not something that happens to us, but something we *do* can help us to realise that we are in control of our lives. It allows us to take more responsibility. We can help the way we feel. We can choose to be grateful.

There are so many things to be grateful for. It could be a relationship, the state of your health, a personal achievement, something related to work or something related to your family or home. There is no limit to what gratitude can be applied to.

Being thankful is all about appreciating what you have and acknowledging its existence in your life. In the fast pace of modern living and the relentless pursuit of materialism, it is so easy to overlook and take for granted what we have – and very often the best things in life are free. For example, your attitude.

One of the premier psychologists of our day is Martin Seligman. Having first gained prominence in researching depression, Seligman soon began to look at factors that contribute to positive emotional health. Seligman's work led to one of the fastest-growing areas of psychological research: "positive psychology". Research has shown that individuals who have a high level of life satisfaction are less likely to have psychological or social problems, less likely to feel stressed, and more likely to enjoy robust physical health.

Seligman and his colleagues have identified 24 key factors associated with individuals who report high levels of life satisfaction. The most recent research suggests that out of these 24, five are particularly important: optimism, zest for life, curiosity, the ability to love and be loved, and gratitude.

It would appear that the most important factor associated with happiness seems to be gratitude. Certainly one theory that proves interesting is that happiness is essentially about shortening the distance between reality and expectation. Clearly, this is not something that the consumerism buys into in its pursuit to make us feel inadequate and insecure!

The average urban dweller is bombarded by well over 1,000 advertisements each day – most of them making us feel dissatisfied with what we have. They suggest that we cannot possibly be happy unless we have the advertised product. I am sure we have all fallen victim to this consumer mentality.

In the midst of this psychological and spiritual junk, gratitude is like a cleansing agent for the soul. It moves us away from what we don't have, to what we do have. The glass stops being half empty and is now half full. Gratitude takes the focus away from self and personal needs. Instead we look at what we have been given; we celebrate the goodness of others.

The word "gratitude" comes from the Latin word *gracia*, which means grace. Rather than living a life filled with stress, anxiety, and striving, gratitude gently teaches us the truth that all life is a gift to be received and enjoyed.

Men and women are not prisoners of fate, but only prisoners of their own minds.

Franklin D. Roosevelt

CHAPTER FIVE

How to be Grateful

*We first make our habits, and then
our habits make us.*

John Dryden

Being grateful, as we have already established, is an attitude. Gratitude is a choice and gratitude, if consciously practised enough, will become a habit. By being grateful for the people, situations and resources around us, we begin to attract better relationships and better personal results. The habit of appreciation will be strengthened as you make the decision to be grateful each and every day.

Here are some useful tips to help you cultivate an attitude of gratitude.

Decide to be grateful

It is entirely your choice whether you want to become a grateful person. If you decide to be a grateful person, then be it. No matter what happens to you, it is still up to you to decide how you want to respond. So *make the decision now* to be a grateful person.

Appreciate life

It is estimated that 106 billion people have been born on Earth, with 6 billion living today. Life expectancy in most of human history is only 20-35 years. And most of those years were spent in disease, poverty, and misery. Only in the last century has human life expectancy increased significantly.

Seek out the good things

Sometimes we see only the bad things that happen in our life and overlook the good things. Open your eyes and be observant of those good things. Dedicate time each day to simply focusing on positive things and seek out something that will make you smile.

Wake up with an attitude of gratitude

You can train your mind to focus on anything you like. When you wake up, you immediately begin to consciously programme your subconscious mind on how your day will be. If you tell yourself that you are going to have a bad or stressful day, then you will, because your subconscious mind will believe anything your conscious mind tells it. Turn any negative thought around and discipline yourself to start every day with a positive and appreciative thought.

Introduce vitamin G

I mentioned at the beginning of the book the concept of vitamin G (vitamin Gratitude). A great way to do this is to have a gratitude stone by your bedside table or by your toothpaste, and remember to take it in your hand each morning and reflect upon what you are grateful for. Do this every day for a month and it will become embedded as a new habit and you will start to notice how good it makes you feel.

Keep a gratitude journal

Take vitamin G one step further and write the good things that happen in your life in a journal, especially those which impress you. When life looks dark and it's difficult for you to be grateful, open and read your journal. Dwelling on the happy positive stuff will help you to realise how wonderful life can be and will be again. This is great to do before you go to bed at night.

See problems as probortunities

Out of every problematic situation there is an opportunity. You can choose to focus on the problem or the solution. This might be difficult for some people – however, I firmly recommend it. At the very least, bad things give you valuable lessons you can be grateful for. When you have this mindset, it's easier to see the good things you can get out of something difficult and challenging. This way you will always have reasons to be grateful.

Hang around radiators

Some people are like drains: they are negative and draining and can zap your energy. Others are like radiators and they can positively warm you with their attitude. Research shows that you can catch other people's negativity germs, and in the same way, positive people can be a tonic. You will become more like the people you are with. Surround yourself with positive people who themselves are grateful people, and it will be much easier and more natural for you to be a grateful person.

Focus on giving

You will be grateful if your mind focuses on what you *have*, rather than what you *don't have*. By *giving*, your mind will focus on what you have, rather than what you don't have (you can't give something you don't have, can you?). Most people focus on *receiving*, which makes their mind focus on what they *don't* have. This is why it's difficult for them to be appreciative.

Get into the habit of saying thank you

Do you always remember to say thank you? Are there times you forget because you are too busy? Perhaps when someone has sent you a gift you haven't let them know how much you appreciated it. Perhaps, when you have been to dinner at someone's house, the next day you forget to let them know how much you enjoyed it. Even the routine things that your family or partner does, do you take it in your stride without acknowledgement? No one likes being taking for granted, so make sure that saying *thank you* is part of the daily fabric of your life.

Say thank you and mean it

Also make sure that saying thank you isn't a chore in your mind. Heartfelt sincere thanks are tangible and not an obligation. When you say thank you to someone, look them in the eyes and mean it! A small gesture like that could make all the difference to someone whose day will glow a little brighter for being acknowledged and appreciated.

Do highlights

Getting into the habit of focusing on the best bits and highlighting three things that made you appreciative and happy is a wonderful way to summarise your day.

For each new morning with its light,
For rest and shelter of the night,
For health and food, for love and friends,
For everything thy goodness sends.

Ralph Waldo Emerson

CHAPTER SIX

What is Happiness?

Happiness is the meaning and the purpose of life, the whole aim and end of human existence.

Aristotle

Being happy is one of our most basic and fundamental desires. We are taught at a very early age that we are to seek out happiness, yet no one really knows what that is. When we are children, our concept of happiness is minimal. As years pass, our concept of happiness becomes much more expansive. We are conditioned to think that, if we succeed at something, whether it is at a career, materially or in relationships, we are seeking to be happy. Some people seek out happiness through religion, or a spiritual leader. It seems that everyone has their own idea as to what makes them happy. It becomes ingrained in us that seeking happiness is the point of our existence.

But how do we really define it? It strikes me that so many people that you meet are looking for happiness. They are on a journey that they hope will take them to this ambrosia-like state. If they are pursuing materialism, they believe that, when they are richer, they will be happier. If they are single, they believe that once they meet someone, they will be happier. If they are on a diet, it's that when they are thinner and look a certain way they will be happier, and so on and so on.

The sad thing is that so many people are missing the opportunity of being happy *right now*. Rather than defining their own definition of happiness, they are seeking approval or justification elsewhere, instead of taking responsibility for redefining the way they perceive happiness and making up their minds to be happier right now. Happiness is within all of us and we are essentially only as happy as we make up our minds to be.

Aristotle, the great philosopher, believed that happiness was the meaning and the purpose of life, the whole aim and end of human existence. Recently, there has been more research on the topic of happiness, and certainly as we have identified having an attitude of gratitude can make us 25% happier.

Happiness isn't a final goal or destination; it is and will always be a work in progress. I rather like the concept of thinking of myself as a person in progress, because I can choose to be content and happy with what I have today and live in hope that every day will add value and that I will aim to improve myself and my engagement with the outside world. Flourishing in our lives and making progress however, requires balance, and living a more wholesome existence that is well rounded and well balanced is key. Having positive emotion and engagement with the world and a sense of meaning and purpose helps us to flourish.

The better we can balance ourselves, the further we can reach. There are so many things that we need to learn to balance these days. For many, the work/home balance can be challenging. With so much temptation around us, balancing some of the excesses can be a constant battle. Perhaps, however, the fundamental balance we need to maintain in our lives is between our two core faculties, which are thoughts and consequently our actions.

We don't think of happiness as a choice, especially when bad luck seems to run through everything we do. But you can choose to be happy, or you can choose negativity. Your choice has a greater influence on your life than you think. When you choose happiness, you lift the spirits of those around you, and you get more happiness in return. If we choose to think that we are happy, this will in turn influence our actions because we will think more about the consequences of what we do. We can ask ourselves: if I do this, will it make me and the people around me happy? These questions need to be asked simultaneously, because if we are doing something that makes us happy and it makes others happy, then we really need to challenge how we derive happiness. A good way to look at this is that, in some way, we are all interconnected, so if we make other people happy, it will make us happy.

You can also help yourself to be happy by deciding every morning that you're in a good mood. Since the day hasn't started yet, nothing has happened to bring you down. Reserve judgement on things you anticipate will be unpleasant or difficult until they've actually happened. It may not turn out as badly as you think, and your positive attitude may just prevent it from happening.

Choose to have a positive attitude even in the face of difficulties. Look for hope in your life. A venture not yet realised or an experience not yet undertaken, but planned, is a reason to be happy. Opportunities are always just around the corner.

Be grateful for the good things you have. Just as life can't always go your way, it can't always go against you, either. Include not just the good people in your life and your accomplishments, but also your positive qualities and what you have to give to the world.

Have faith in what life brings, because life has a strange way of giving gifts when we least expect it. Be open to receiving success, happiness and joy and let yourself enjoy the positive experiences of your life without hesitation.

In April 2011, a new movement was launched called Action For Happiness. There is more information about this movement at the end of the book. I strongly recommend you visit the website www.actionfor happiness.org as it is full of wonderful information and inspiration.

Happiness really is a fascinating subject and, it would seem, an increasingly topical subject, as wellbeing is a far more examined area especially with the increase in depression and mental health issues. Having explored the whole concept of happiness during the research for my previous book, the resounding conclusion I came to was that the ultimate definition of happiness is unique to each individual. You define your own happiness and it isn't *out there* – it's already inside and if you don't feel it now, it's because you haven't woken it up yet.

"Happiness is itself a kind of gratitude."

Joseph Wood Krutch

CHAPTER SEVEN

Be Your Own Best Friend

When you feel good about yourself,
others will feel good about you, too.

Jake Steinfeld

So let's take a good look at YOU, or rather, why don't you take a good look at yourself and start by being really honest. What is your opinion of yourself? Are you appreciative of all your strengths and qualities, or do you beat yourself up on a regular basis about all your misgivings, mistakes and weaknesses?

If it is the latter, I am sure that you would not consciously treat anyone else, let alone your best friend, that way so why do we do it to ourselves? Why are we sometimes our own worst enemy?

It is amazing how so many people, when you compliment them for something you admire, will almost reject the compliment rather than simply saying thank you and allowing themselves to feel the benefits of being appreciated.

Lack of self-appreciation is one of the reasons people become depressed. Appreciating yourself is the most important component of self-love. However that sounds, it is hugely important, because if we don't love ourselves, why would we even begin to expect anyone else to? People who appreciate themselves usually have a good heart and are full of optimism. They love and appreciate the gifts that they have bestowed upon them. They feel comfortable in themselves and are known for their generosity and tolerance.

The expression of appreciation is essential for your emotional health and well-being. Appreciation is a skill that we can all learn. However, it must start at home. It has to start with an appreciation of yourself.

We have to take responsibility for being the best that we can be. So often we will compare ourselves to others, and if we do this, we run the danger of engendering two emotions: one of vanity or one of bitterness, because there will always be people we see as better or worse off than ourselves. It is also pointless to benchmark ourselves against others – using ourselves as our own benchmark is far more constructive. Strive to be the best YOU can be.

My sister Jacky Pearson (www.jackypearson.com - I feel I must add her website for people who love and appreciate art, so they don't miss out!) is a wonderfully talented watercolour artist who lives in New Zealand. When I first started writing, I lacked confidence in my ability to be as good as other writers, and she said that she had felt the same about her art. But she decided that she would no longer allow herself to do this, and her focus and ambition would be about being a better artist than she had been the year before, and use this as her goal and herself as her own benchmark. This was a great piece of advice, and certainly helps take away the weight of pressure that we so unnecessarily put upon ourselves.

We are essentially driven by two things: fear and desire. If we are not careful, we can allow fear to stop us trying new things, just in case we make a mistake. However, for every mistake that you make, another valuable lesson is learnt. So, on a very positive note, you are building your pot of wisdom.

Working on your own self-confidence is key. There is a fine line between arrogance and confidence, and it is important to be honest with yourself and seek feedback from others. It is also important, however, that you don't rely on others to big you up and make you feel better. It is important that you learn how to recognise and appreciate yourself when you have done something well. If you rely on others or become so preoccupied with others' opinions of you, it can create insecurity and paranoia.

Imagine having no one to compare yourself with except yourself. What a sense of relief this would bring. We wouldn't have to worry about not looking like the alpha male or female with the smartest mind, the most important job role and the biggest pay packet. We wouldn't have to worry about our bodies not being the youngest, most beautiful and most sexy.

All we would have to think is: did I do this activity better than I did it last week? Have I moved forward in my own definition of success? Am I feeling peaceful; doing my best for my health? Do I have an attractive mind and healthy interactions with other people?

Many of us would never admit to making comparisons with other people – to do so implies jealousy and small-mindedness. However, everyone has undoubtedly taken a measure of themselves at some point by reference to someone else – even if only subconsciously.

Being the best that we can be is the most realistic ambition. We are essentially people in progress. I like this concept. It means that we can always improve, and as long as we head in the right direction with the right intention, then every breath we take is a breath worth taking.

Here is a short exercise that will help you on the road to appreciating yourself and learning how to be your own best friend.

Five things I like about myself

1.

2.

3.

4.

5.

Five things I do that add value to the world around me

1.

2.

3.

4.

5.

My proudest achievement in the last 12 months is ....

To learn how to appreciate yourself, you have to know your positive qualities. If there is something that you don't like, then work on changing it. You must know that you have many good things to offer to humanity, so begin to trust and appreciate yourself.

You yourself, as much as anybody in the entire universe, deserve your love and affection.

Buddha

CHAPTER EIGHT

**it Happens

*Reflect upon your present blessings, of which
every man has plenty; not on your past
misfortunes of which all men have some.*

Charles Dickens

**it happens – or perhaps a slightly more eloquent term
would be *c'est la vie*. Both are the acknowledgement
that life is full of imperfections and not everything
always goes according to plan. As someone once said to
me, "You can't always have it your own way; sometimes
you are the bird and sometimes you are the statue!"

The pleasure-pain principle is very useful because, if
we don't ever experience pain, then how can we
evaluate and appreciate pleasure? Life happens and so
do a whole raft of things, and some of them can be very
challenging. All life experiences can enrich us if we
reflect upon them in a positive way. Even out of
extreme crisis situations, there is always opportunity
and learning.

If we choose, however, to focus on all the negative
aspects of the past and spend each day dragging them up
and reliving them, then we will end up feeling miserable.

One day I was agonising over a decision that I had made to my friend Sassy, who listened to me patiently and then said, "Stop 'should'-ing on yourself", and I realised that so much of what I was saying was about what I could have, would have, should have done. True, reflection can be useful in terms of learning from the past; however, staying too long in a dwelling, regretful state can be counterproductive and unnecessarily self-indulgent.

I would also challenge the concept of *burying the past*. The danger with this is that we will then go back at a later stage and dig it up. Acknowledging past negative experiences, learning from them and then consciously letting them go is by far the healthiest approach.

Some people have a propensity to live in the past and kick things around for ages; however, there comes a point where letting go is the best way to move on without the shackles of regret. There is a great acronym, SUMO – it means Shut Up Move On!

There are several different forms of cognitive (thinking) activity, some conscious and some unconscious, that can also be useful here.

The type of conscious cognitive activity that is quickest to yield results is to control what is known as your "self-talk". As I mentioned before, we have about 60,000-80,000 thoughts every day – that is a lot of internal dialogue.

Listening to yourself is one of the most powerful life skills you can possess. It is important to challenge your thoughts – are they helpful? What kinds of things are you saying to yourself?

Your Reticular Activating System (RAS) is a wonderfully evolved part of your brain that is a filter between your conscious and your subconscious. It takes instructions from your conscious mind and passes them on to your subconscious.

So why does it do this? We are literally bombarded with sensory images, sounds and goings on all day long. Just imagine what your life would be like if you were aware of every single one of them – it would be mental bedlam! The RAS consists of a bundle of densely packed nerve cells located in the central core of the brainstem. Roughly the size of a little finger, the RAS runs from the top of the spinal cord into the middle of the brain. This area of tightly-packed nerve fibres and cells contain nearly 70% of your brain's nerve cells.

The RAS acts as the executive secretary for your conscious mind. It is the chief gatekeeper that screens or filters the type of information that will be allowed to get through. The great thing is that YOU control it. IT doesn't control you – so at a conscious level, you can programme it any way you like.

Another trigger for depression and anxiety is catastrophising – worrying about something that hasn't happened yet and might not happen at all. Worry, by its very nature, means thinking about the future, and comes from the Anglo-Saxon word *wyrgan*, which literally means to strangle and choke until there is no life left.

Worry, as a stressor, is a direct source of headaches, insomnia, ulcers and other gastric distress, paranoia, generalised anxiety disorders, depression and phobias.

Worry is the mental counterpart of anxiety, although worry often includes angry thoughts and images. That is to say, we worry about the things we fear may happen.

It is very important to acknowledge that what we do consciously affects the subconscious, as well – so in considering worry, we know that we can identify and control our worries, and that by controlling our conscious worry, we can affect the reservoir of anxiety that our worry has left behind in our subconscious.

We all have ongoing internal dialogues about concerns, hopes, plans, decisions and so forth, and we can easily observe what we're saying to ourselves, how we're saying it, when we're saying it and what our perspectives and intentions are. Worry involves a great deal of self-talk. Controlling worry can be easily accomplished by intentionally intervening and having a little chat with yourself.

When you are worried about something, you are having distressing conversations with yourself about things you imagine might happen. You are, however, literally worried about nothing. These imagined events are in your mind, not in your real, physical environment

– there is nothing you can do about the objects of your worry. You are stuck. You are helpless. You can't do anything about nothing.

You can, however, intervene in these self-abusive internal dialogues as if you were an outside, objective mediator. You can transform these dialogues into useful and productive activities that allay the fears you feel.

One technique I find useful is to say "Stop" in your mind. Mentally shout it, if necessary. Whenever you find yourself worrying, stop the dialogue this way immediately. This may sound too easy, but it really works!

Next, replace the worry dialogue with a practical dialogue. The events you are anticipating really might occur and you can't waste your time stuck in the worry cycle. You have to plan your most effective responses. You have to determine if there is anything you can do right now to prevent or modify those events. Talk to yourself about what might happen and what you could do about it. Write it down if this helps.

Another technique I use if I can't sleep is to take a sheet of paper and write down all the things I am anxious about and then write down what the best possible outcome could be. Turning worries around in your mind can be so helpful.

I have known a great many troubles,
but most of them never happened.

Mark Twain

CHAPTER NINE

The Gift of Now

The past is history

The future a mystery

Today is a gift

That's why it's called the present

The Wise Tortoise - Kung Fu Panda

If you're too busy dwelling on the past or thinking about the future, you won't be able to fully appreciate the moment and notice all the good things around you. Also, dwelling on the past and thinking about the future opens the door to comparison, which is the only way you can perceive something as not good enough. What you have now is all that exists, and comparing that to something that doesn't exist anymore (or yet) is an easy way to foster dissatisfaction.

Research indicates that living in the moment can make people happier, because most negative thoughts concern the past or the future. If you hoist yourself into the awareness of the present moment, worrying melts away. Savouring the here and now forces you into the present, so you can't worry about things that aren't there.

With the fast pace of modern life, it isn't always easy to slow down and appreciate the moment. When people are not in the moment, they're not there to know that they're not there, if you see what I mean! Overriding the distraction reflex and awakening to the present takes intentionality and practice.

Cultivating a nonjudgemental awareness of the present can bring a whole host of benefits. Mindfulness as a state of living in the moment can boost immune functioning, reduce pain, lower blood pressure, and reduce stress, which is one of the increasingly common conditions of modern living.

People who can appreciate the moment are happier, more exuberant, more empathetic, and more secure. They have higher self-esteem and are more accepting of their own weaknesses. Anchoring awareness in the here and now can reduce the kind of reactivity that underlies depression, binge eating, and attention-deficit disorders.

I have to say that I, for one, have not always found the mindful state easy to achieve especially as I have the creative mind of a butterfly. However, once mastered (and it takes a lot of practice) it is a very useful skill, especially if you are challenged with anxiety or depression. It's amazing how much you can miss when you are not in the present. Technology doesn't help and mobile phones are one of the biggest culprits for distracting us from the here and now and what is around us. They are highly unsociable too, because, when you want to make someone feel appreciated, it is important to be with them in full attendance.

As my friend Jacky pointed out to me as I was texting quite a bit during an evening out with a group of friends, "It would be great if you could join us tonight!" Fair comment. Sometimes we just don't even realise how far we are removed from the here and now and what is around us. Technology certainly seems to compound that as we all become slaves to our various mobile gadgets!

Perhaps the most complete way of living in the moment is the state of total absorption that psychologists call *flow*. Flow occurs when you're so engrossed in a task that you lose track of everything else around you. Flow embodies an apparent paradox: How can you be living in the moment if you're not even aware of the moment? The depth of engagement absorbs you powerfully, keeping attention so focused that distractions cannot penetrate. You focus so intensely on what you're doing that you're unaware of the passage of time. Hours can pass without you noticing.

Flow is an elusive state. As with romance or sleep, you can't just will yourself into it – all you can do is set the stage, creating the optimal conditions for it to occur.

Flow is when you feel as if your awareness merges with the action you're performing. You feel a sense of personal mastery over the situation, and the activity is so intrinsically rewarding that, although the task is difficult, action feels effortless.

You can become mindful at any time you like just by paying attention to your immediate experience and situation. You can do it right now. What's happening this instant? Think of yourself as an external observer, and just observe the moment. What do you see, hear, smell? Without judging how it feels, just absorb what is around you – and if you notice your mind wandering, bring yourself back. Just keep focusing on the moment.

Here are a few tips to help you.

✓ Stop and look around. Notice beautiful shapes, colours, and details. Notice things you normally take for granted, like sunlight reflecting off someone's hair. Think of all the little things you'd miss if you were blind. It's often the most minute joys that are missed the most.
✓ Smell the roses. And the food. And the air. Recognise the smells that make you feel good: a freshly cut lawn, the air right after it rains, a fresh pot of coffee.
✓ Savour your food, slowly. Enjoy. Identify flavours. Appreciate how they intermingle. Take notes from wine enthusiasts; they know how to enjoy the subtlest of flavours.
✓ Appreciate the sense of touch. How do leaves, blankets, lotions feel against your skin? How many times during the day do people touch you affectionately, and you barely notice?
✓ Listen to more than music. Listen when you think it's quiet, and you'll discover it's not really all that quiet. You might hear the wind; leaves rustling, people laughing.

Imagine if time was a bank account and, each morning, you were credited with 86,400 seconds. If, by the end of that day, you hadn't spent any of the credits, they would instantly be deducted from your account. What would you do? You would most likely try to use every one of them. So enjoy each second of every minute of every hour of every day, because the moment is something that we can never recover.

Look to this day, the very life of life,
In its brief course lies all,
The realities and varieties of existence,
The bliss of growth, the splendour of action,
The glory of power.
For yesterday is but a dream,
And tomorrow is only a vision.
But today well lived, makes every yesterday
A dream of happiness
And every tomorrow
A vision of hope.
Look well, therefore,
To this day.

Sanskrit Proverb

CHAPTER TEN

Greet the Day

*When you arise in the morning, think of
what a precious privilege it is to be alive,
to breathe, to think, to enjoy, to love.*

Marcus Aurelius

When I was little, my father used to come into my room in the morning full of the joys of spring (even in winter) and open the curtains and say, "Are you ready to greet the day?" Whenever I go to visit my parents, he still does this, armed with a cup of tea and a big smile. Both my parents, who are now in their late seventies and in retirement, wouldn't dream of lounging about in bed in the morning and wasting the day away.

An early morning start is the best way to begin appreciating your day. In the words of the Dalai Lama:

"Every day, think as you wake up, 'Today I am fortunate to have woken up, I am alive, I have a precious human life, I am not going to waste it. I am going to use all my energies to develop myself, to expand my heart out to others, to achieve enlightenment for the benefit of all beings, I am going to have kind thoughts towards

others, I am not going to get angry or think badly about others, I am going to benefit others as much as I can.' "

One tip that I have picked up along the way is to "refuse the snooze". Let's face it, sometimes it is so tempting to press the snooze button and to snuggle up under the warmth and comfort of our duvets again and drift back into a semi-slumber. However, this is not the best way to start the day. Waking up and getting up to appreciate what the day has in store will bring you far more treasures.

Here are some of the benefits of getting up early:

- ✓ The early morning hours are so peaceful and so quiet and a perfect time for setting the scene for your day ahead.
- ✓ It will allow you thinking time. This is really important in the fast-paced world that we find ourselves living in – we do not give ourselves permission to have some really good quality thinking time.
- ✓ This will allow you time to take your daily dose of vitamin G (gratitude) and you will have time to reinforce in your mind all the things you are grateful for.
- ✓ This time could also be spent writing your gratitude journal, if you find yourself too tired to do it the evening before.
- ✓ People who wake late miss one of the greatest feats of nature, the rising of the sun (on sunny days!)
- ✓ Rise early and you actually have time for breakfast, which is the most important meal of the day.

Without breakfast, your body is running on fumes, until you are so hungry at lunchtime that you eat whatever unhealthy thing you can find.

✓ Exercising in the morning is a great way to start the day, whether this is a lovely early morning stroll, a trip to the gym, meditation, yoga or whatever you enjoy.

✓ Mornings are the best time to set goals and organise your day by sorting out your priorities set your priority list for the day. It's a good way to organise your day and get the best out of it.

✓ You will be able to factor a bit of extra "you" time in before the rest of the world starts to make its demands upon you.

✓ You will find that, by giving yourself some extra time, you won't find yourself rushing around playing catch-up and your stress levels will be far better managed.

So, if you struggle with being an early riser, here are few tips that will help you:

✓ Don't make drastic changes. Start slowly, by waking just 15-30 minutes earlier than usual. Get used to this for a few days. Then cut back another 15 minutes. Do this gradually until you get to your goal time.

✓ Make a conscious decision to go to bed earlier. You might be used to staying up late watching TV but if you continue this habit while trying to get up earlier, sooner or later one is going to give.

✓ Refuse the snooze. Position your alarm clock far from your bed. If it's right next to your bed, you'll shut it off or hit snooze. It's the best way to get up and get going!

✓ Use self-talk to tell you that getting up is far more beneficial than lying in bed and wasting the precious early morning moments.

✓ Set something to do early in the morning that's important. This will motivate you to get up.

✓ Make sure you take advantage of all that extra time. Keep a log of all the extra things you do as a result of waking up early. This will be a great way to remind yourself when you read it back of the benefits of greeting the day.

There is no snooze button on a cat
who wants breakfast.

Author Unknown

CHAPTER ELEVEN

Live Well

If I'd known I was going to live so long, I'd have taken better care of myself.

Leon Eldred

I have a small plaque on my bathroom wall that I look at every day, and it says:

Live Well – Laugh Often – Love Much

The next three chapters look at each of these concepts in turn. I am a firm believer that positive living requires a holistic approach and all aspects of life need to be nurtured in order to get the right balance . These three areas create the foundation to help you to appreciate your life more.

First of all it is really important to look after yourself physically through a healthy lifestyle because your health is your wealth.

In almost every country, the proportion of people aged over 60 years is growing faster than any other age group. Data from the Continuous Mortality Investigation shows that while a 65-year-old male might, in 1997, have expected to die at 83, the figure for 2005 was over 86, and the projected figure for 2015 is nearly 90. On that basis, taking personal responsibility and caring for our health is becoming increasingly important if we are to enjoy and appreciate our retirement.

It's interesting the way people spend so much time focusing on the necessity for material security as they get older and yet don't always consider the investment they make in their own health bank. Perhaps that is because the state of our health is less visible to us than the state of our bank accounts. But treating our bodies like a pension is so important.

When we are younger, we take our bodies for granted, not really bearing in mind the ramifications that will inevitably occur later in our lives. While you may have secured the best material pension, can you honestly say that you have given your health the same level of positive investment?

There are so many conflicting bits of advice about what good health is and the media hypes and manipulates the evidence to fit the needs of the consumer bandwagon. One minute something is really bad for us; the next, it is good. What are we to believe? Having researched nutrition for my book *How to Work Wonders – Your Guide to Workplace Wellness*, I was fascinated with the conflicting evidence I discovered. I am not surprised that so many people get confused about what a healthy, balanced diet looks like.

One thing that I have come to believe is that good health is about balance, not necessarily abstinence. A little bit of everything in moderation (except smoking and drugs of course!).

So here are a few basic tips and advice that will help you to promote better health, so that you can invest in your future wellbeing. None of this is rocket science and quite frankly you probably know most of it – however it isn't what you know it's what you do with it!

Eat a balanced diet – A nutritious breakfast is so important to sustain your energy levels throughout the morning, followed by a high-protein lunch containing only a small amount of good quality carbohydrates. High carbs such as white bread or pasta produce sleep-inducing hormones, which will result in lethargy and bloating in the afternoons. There is a great adage that says: "Breakfast like a king – Lunch like a prince – Dinner like a pauper". Also don't forget your five a day of fruit and vegetables.

Energy in - Energy Out – Faddy diets do not work! A healthy diet for life is by far the best approach. Most men need about 2,500 calories a day and most women 2,000 calories a day. If you exercise, you can eat more. It really is a simple mathematical equation when it comes to losing or putting on weight: calories that you consume versus calories you expend.

Cut down on sugar – Refined sugar has 90% of its vitamins and minerals removed. Without sufficient vitamins and minerals, our metabolism becomes inefficient, contributing to poor health and weight management issues. Sugary foods can also compromise your immune system. Research has shown that white blood cells are less efficient at fighting illness when exposed to refined sugar. A diet high in refined sugar will also raise your insulin levels quickly, which can lead to many other health problems. You will also lack energy as a result of these sugar spikes and the drop in blood sugar that follows.

Exercise – Buy a pedometer and get walking. Walking is one of the best forms of exercise: walking 10,000 steps a day is great for the heart and mind and can have the same effect according to research as a mild antidepressant. To feel instantly revived, march on the spot, run up and down stairs, skip or dance for a minute or two. Your circulation will increase oxygen to the brain.

Get lots of fresh air – As stale air encourages stagnation, work and sleep in a room where you can open the window. If this is not possible, take short breaks throughout the day and walk outside. Take deep breaths of fresh air to rejuvenate the system.

Drink two litres of water a day – Water is liquid energy and, in my opinion, has magical properties! Both mental and physical performance is affected when the brain is only 3% dehydrated. Herbal teas can also be drunk; however, tea and coffee are not a good substitute, because too much caffeine can have a diuretic effect.

Alcohol – Whilst alcohol is very nice and has become very much part of our social fabric, it is important not to overindulge too often. It is important to stick to the government guidelines, which indicate 2 small units a day for women and 3 small units for men. There are many websites now that will help you track your alcohol consumption.

Caffeine – Avoid too much tea or coffee. A recommended amount is no more than two cups of coffee or three cups of tea. You can drink as much herbal tea as you like. Green tea is great for energy. Do beware fizzy drinks – some are loaded with caffeine and artificial sweeteners.

Quality Sleep – The quality of your sleep is so important, and a good 6-8 hours is recommended. Avoid caffeine or any stimulants before you go to bed. A cup of camomile tea can be very good for promoting sleep, too.

Most of this is very basic advice. However, it is really important to ensure that you cultivate a lifestyle that promotes healthy habits. As we now live so much longer than ever before, it is becoming increasingly important that we take more personal responsibility for our health, so that we can fully appreciate long, healthy and happy lives.

The part can never be well unless the whole is well.

Plato

Chapter Twelve

Laugh Often

*Laughter is the shock absorber that
eases the blows of life.*

Author Unknown

Laughter is one of the best antidotes for reducing the day to day stress and anxiety that so many of us in this day and age experience, and has proven to be an extremely effective way to increase the positive energy that is responsible and necessary for achieving happiness.

Appreciating the humour in some situations has proven to be a powerful antidote to depression. When I was in America a few years ago, I attended a laughter clinic, which was fascinating. Some organisations now use these clinics in the workplace to help alleviate stress.

Laughter is found in various animals, as well as in humans. Among the human race, it is a part of human behaviour regulated by the brain, helping humans to clarify their intentions in social interaction and providing an emotional context to conversations. Laughter is used as a signal for being part of a group, and it can signal acceptance and positive interactions with others. Laughter is sometimes seemingly contagious, and the laughter of one person can have a great impact on others.

Scientifically speaking, laughter is caused by the epiglottis constricting the larynx, causing respiratory upset, which in itself sounds a funny way to describe it. For any of you who may one day get the quiz question, just for your information, the study of humour and laughter is called gelotology.

Laughter is a mechanism that everyone has; laughter is part of universal human vocabulary. There are thousands of languages, hundreds of thousands of dialects, but everyone speaks laughter in pretty much the same way. Everyone can laugh. Babies have the ability to laugh before they ever speak. Children who are born blind and deaf still retain the ability to laugh.

Scientific research demonstrates that laughter has the following health benefits:

- ✓ Lowering blood pressure
- ✓ Strengthening cardiovascular functions
- ✓ Reducing stress hormones
- ✓ Improving circulation
- ✓ Increasing muscle flexion
- ✓ Oxygenating the body by boosting the respiratory system
- ✓ Boosting immune function by raising levels of infection-fighting T-cells

✓ Triggering the release of endorphins, the body's natural painkillers
✓ Producing a general sense of well-being

Here are a few ways to promote your sense of humour:

Smile

Smiling is the gateway to laughter and smiling, like laughter, is also contagious. Start off by smiling at simple things, and make a conscious effort to smile more often. Other than making you feel good, smiling also makes you attractive. People are naturally drawn to people who smile easily, and a smile can change your mood and helps you to feel positive.

Smiling is also a natural drug, and when you smile, your body releases endorphins and serotonin. Endorphins are also known as the body's natural feel-good chemicals or natural painkillers. Serotonin is a hormone that is found naturally in the human brain. It is known as a "happy" hormone, because it influences an overall sense of well-being. Serotonin also plays a part in regulating moods, tempering anxiety, and relieving depression – so a whole host of benefits here!

Avoid toxic people

Some people can be really quite toxic for the soul; others like a tonic, so seeking to spend time with fun, playful and positive people is a great way to embrace humour. Tonic people laugh easily and they can find humour in almost everything in everyday events, even in a bad situation. They observe the world through the eyes of exaggeration and a silly perspective and don't take life or themselves too seriously.

Entertain yourself

Watching comedy shows and funny films or going along to stand-up comedy clubs is an instant way to attract humour. Have a good belly laugh, as laughter encourages your intake of oxygen-rich air and stimulates your heart, lungs and muscles. Enjoy the humour and the beneficial effects on your body and mind at the same time. Another great source of humour is reading cartoon strips and jokes from your daily papers or magazines or buying a book of jokes or funny uplifting stories.

Grow down

We spend our lives being told to "grow up" and then when you reach adulthood, you realise that being like a child again is a great way to appreciate the funny things in life. One scientific experiment found that children laugh up to 300 times a day, whereas the average adult laughs 20 times a day. When you observe children, they throw caution to the wind and take life lightly and laugh at just about anything. They sing aloud and dance with no embarrassment or reason. So sometimes it's good to grow down, rather than up! Feel like a child again and recharge your life.

Remember, **a day without laughter is a day wasted.** So liven up, start laughing today and live a long and healthy life.

What soap is to the body, laughter is to the soul.

Yiddish Proverb

CHAPTER THIRTEEN

Love Much

Being deeply loved by someone gives
you strength, while loving someone
deeply gives you courage.

Lao Tzu

I have to say I love the whole topic of "love", and I am just in the process of doing some research for one of my next books, which is going to be about this somewhat nebulous subject. Defining love is not dissimilar to trying to define happiness or our purpose in life. It means so many different things to different people. Love is any one of a number of emotions and experiences related to a sense of strong affection and attachment to something or someone.

The word *love* can refer to a variety of different feelings, states, and attitudes, ranging from generic pleasure to intense interpersonal attraction. This diversity of uses and meanings, combined with the complexity of the feelings involved, makes love unusually difficult to define consistently, even compared to other emotional states. It has been cited, however, as one of the most evocative ways to appreciate life.

As a purely abstract concept, *love* usually refers to a deep feeling of tenderly caring for another person. Even this conception of love, however, encompasses a wealth of different feelings, from the passionate desire and intimacy of romantic love to the non - sexual emotional closeness of familial and platonic love to the profound devotion of religious love.

Love, in its various forms, acts as a major facilitator of interpersonal relationships and, owing to its central psychological importance, is one of the most common themes in the creative arts. Plays, books and most song lyrics are devoted to the subject.

Love can bring along a great deal of pleasure and in turn a great deal of pain. Unrequited love and disrespected love can break hearts and confuse minds. We can love someone intensely, but it may be that we don't love the person we have to become in order to do that. Love can be used as a weapon or a healing agent. It is an incredibly powerful emotion.

In a classic book by John Lee, entitled *Colors of Love*, six varieties of relationship that might be labelled as love were defined and these included the following:

Eros – A passionate physical and emotional love based on aesthetic enjoyment; stereotype of romantic love.

Ludus – A love that is played as a game, sport or conquest and may feature multiple partners at once.

Storge – An affectionate love that slowly develops from friendship, based on similarity and desire to share.

Pragma – A love that is driven by the head, not the heart, and is fundamentally undemonstrative.

Mania – Obsessive love; experiencing great emotional highs and lows; very possessive and often jealous lovers.

Agape – Selfless altruistic and spiritual love.

The experience of love for a life partner or soul mate could be divided into three partly overlapping stages, which include lust, attraction, and attachment.

The first is an initial passionate sexual desire that promotes mating, and involves the increased release of chemicals such as testosterone and oestrogen. These effects rarely last more than a few weeks or months. Attraction is the more individualised and romantic desire for a specific candidate for mating, which develops out of lust as commitment to an individual mate forms. Recent studies in neuroscience have indicated that, as people fall in love, the brain consistently releases a certain set of chemicals, including pheromones, dopamine, norepinephrine, and serotonin, which act in a manner similar to amphetamines, stimulating the brain's centre and leading to side effects such as increased heart rate, loss of appetite and sleep, and an intense feeling of excitement.

The lust and attraction stages are both considered temporary, and a third stage is needed to account for long-term relationships. Attachment is the bonding that promotes relationships lasting for many years and even decades. Attachment is generally based on commitments such as marriage and children, or on mutual friendship based on things like shared interests. It has been linked to higher levels of the chemicals oxytocin and vasopressin to a greater degree than short-term relationships have.

My favourite description of romantic love is from the book *Captain Corelli's Mandolin* by Louis de Bernières.

There is a passage that describes falling in love as a temporary madness and goes something like this: Falling in love is like an earthquake, it erupts, and then it subsides and when it subsides, you have to make a decision. You have to work out whether your roots have become so entwined together that it is inconceivable that you should ever part. Because this is what love is. Love is not breathlessness, it is not excitement, it is not the desire to make love every second of the day. That is just being in love; which any of us can convince ourselves that we are. Love itself is what is left over, when being in love has burned away.

My parents have been together for sixty years and happily married for nearly fifty-eight. I asked my father one day what their secret to success was in a world where so many relationships don't stand the test of time.

"Silence", he told me.

When I probed him further for an explanation, he said: "Well, it's simple, really – when your mother is in the wrong, I don't say anything, and when I am in the right, I don't say anything!"

He also said that once he hadn't spoken to my mother for a week. When I asked him why, he said,"I didn't want to interrupt her!"

Something I have observed with my parents is that when it comes to love, appreciation of each other's strengths, an unconditional tolerance of each other's quirky bits and a good sense of humour can be what transforms a good relationship into a wonderful one!

At the touch of love everyone becomes a poet.

Plato

CHAPTER FOURTEEN

Be Kind

My religion is very simple. My religion is kindness.

Dalai Lama

When I was about ten, my grandmother told me a story about kindness.

It is called *The Wise Woman's Stone*.

One day a wise woman was travelling in the mountains, where she found a precious stone in a stream. The next day, she met another traveller who was hungry, and the wise woman opened her bag to share her food with him.

The hungry traveller saw the precious stone and asked the woman to give it to him. She did so immediately and without any hesitation, even though she knew how valuable it was. The traveller left, rejoicing in his good fortune. He knew the stone was worth enough to give him security for a lifetime. However, a few days later he came back to return the stone to the wise woman.

"I've been thinking," he said, "I know how valuable the stone is, but I want to give it back in the hope that you can give me something even more precious."

"What is that?" the wise woman asked.

"Please can you give me what you have within you that enabled you to give me the stone."

That story always makes me tingle, as does any act of kindness. Helping others takes all sorts of forms and springs from countless motivations, from deep-rooted empathy to a more calculated desire for public recognition. Social scientists have identified a host of ways in which charitable behaviour can lead to benefits for the giver.

Being grateful for what we have is so important with regards to creating and sustaining the feel-good factor. Helping others can also make us happier and healthier, too. Studies show that helping others can boost happiness and increases life satisfaction, providing a sense of meaning, increasing feelings of competence, improving our mood and reducing stress. It can also help to take our minds off our own troubles.

Doing things for others, whether it's just a very small thing or spontaneous gestures or regular planned volunteering, is a powerful way to boost our own happiness as well as those around us.

Giving isn't just about money, as some people may believe, so you don't need to wait until you win the lottery! Giving to others can be as simple as some words and compliments, a smile or a thoughtful gesture. It can include giving time, care, skills, thought or attention. Sometimes these can mean more than any financial gestures.

Giving also connects us to others, creating stronger communities and helping to build a happier society for everyone.

Kindness and caring also seem to be contagious. When we see someone do something kind or thoughtful, or we are on the receiving end of kindness, it inspires us to be kinder ourselves. In this way, kindness spreads from one person to the next, influencing the behaviour of people who never saw the original act.

Kindness really is the key to creating a happier, more trusting world. While it has long been assumed that giving also leads to greater happiness, this has only recently started to be scientifically proven.

Human beings are highly social creatures and have evolved as a species living with others. If people are altruistic, they are more likely to be liked and in turn build better social connections and stronger and more supportive social networks, which leads to increased feelings of happiness and well-being.

Giving literally feels good.

It used to be thought that human beings only did things when they got something in return. How, then, could we explain people who performed kind acts or donated money anonymously? Studies of the brain now show that when we give money to good causes, the same parts of the brain light up as if we were receiving money ourselves (or responding to other pleasurable stimuli, such as food, money or sex). Giving to others activates the reward centres of our brains, which make us feel good and so encourages us to do more of the same. Giving money to a good cause literally feels as good as receiving it, especially if the donations are voluntary.

Giving help has a stronger association with mental health than receiving it. Studies have shown that volunteers have fewer symptoms of depression and anxiety and they feel more hopeful. It is also related to feeling good about oneself. It can serve to distract people from dwelling on their own problems and be grateful for what they have.

There are so many ways that we can learn to give and this is a behaviour that can be learned and practised and become part of the fabric of our everyday lives.

We make a living by what we get.
We make a life by what we give.

Winston Churchill

CHAPTER FIFTEEN

Family Matters

*Families are like fudge - mostly sweet
with a few nuts.*

Author Unknown

I am sure you may have heard the expression that, "You can choose your friends, but you can't choose your family". However, you can choose the relationship you have with your family. It's easier to take your family for granted than it is your friends, and very often we can be a lot less tolerant and compassionate around our family than we are with our friends.

The word family derives from the Latin *familiar,* and the old adage that familiarity breeds contempt, sadly, for some families, can be true. Frequently, you hear about upsets and discontent in families and a whole host of long-term feuds and grudges.

I dare say we all experience problems with our families from time to time, some more than others. Whether we are living together or apart, we may have family members whom we feel interfere or control too much. Perhaps they judge and criticise. Perhaps there is sibling rivalry and petty jealousies that exist or lazy relatives who take advantage of other family members.

One thing to consider is that, whatever the situation, they are your one and only family, your gift at birth, so why not make the best of what you have? It really is important to put just as much effort into your family as you do your friends.

The most important first step to learning how to appreciate them more is to stop trying to change them and work with their strengths, rather than focusing on their weaknesses. The danger we run in any kind of relationship is when we start trying to change people, rather than celebrating and accepting who they are. No one is perfect – for every strength we possess, we will have an allowable weakness or limitation. Accepting in yourself and everyone else around you will allow you to release any frustrations you try to harness. It is very unlikely that you will change anyone, so the best approach is to change your attitude and see the positive in everyone.

Making an extra effort can make all the difference. If you really want harmony in the family, perhaps just taking that first step is all it takes. If two people are stubbornly fighting with each other and one decides not to argue anymore, it leaves room for change.

We all have quirks and habits that will annoy and irritate people, but bear in mind that what annoys or irritates us about someone else is very often what we don't really like about ourselves. Tolerance and a pound of empathy can carry us a long way in creating harmonious relationships.

Each person's well-being and happiness can be supported and nurtured by their family. Unfortunately, most people tend to neglect their families, especially when busy pursuing their career or other activities.

What some people can forget and overlook in their busy lives is to spend quality time with the people they love. Family is the prime factor that helps most people succeed in their careers. For this reason, it is vital that there should always be a balance between work and family.

Today's competitive world makes work very demanding and stressful. It does not only mean meeting deadlines and handling projects, but the schedule in itself can be very hectic and it is important not to bring stress home.

Stress can be eliminated if you spend quality time with your children and loved ones at home. The very fact that you will be surrounded with their laughter and love can already take away the stress that has been with you at work. It simply invigorates your mind and well-being as a whole. Leisure time spent with your family is the perfect time for you to become fresh and energised, which ultimately helps people to work better.

Every time you spend quality time with your family, you are allowing better communication. You get to understand them better by learning what they like or need. The time you spend with your family will simply strengthen your relationship and the love you share.

For this reason, it is very important that one should balance life at home and at work. Having your family at your side supporting you will give you the strength to surpass all challenges life brings.

Here are a few tips to help you appreciate your family more and develop healthier and happier relationships:

- ✓ Spend quality time with your family and be present with them when you are with them.
- ✓ Learn to be positive about your family and seek out and celebrate the things that you like about them.
- ✓ Learn about them as "people" and take an interest in what they do, what they know and how they actually feel.
- ✓ Respect and try to see their point of view as you would anyone else.
- ✓ If you are upset about something, talk about it, don't just bury it under the carpet and hope it will go away – it won't, you will just find yourself sitting on a pile of dust.
- ✓ Have a sense of humour and find the funny side of situations so your home environment is light and happy.
- ✓ Be careful about bringing your own stress into the home and family environment and take personal responsibility for your emotions.
- ✓ Don't have the TV on every night. Play games, make things; talk.

✓ Ask each other questions and really listen to the answers.

✓ Try to get out in the evenings and go for a walk together.

✓ At the end of the day, do "Highlights": share with each other the best three things that have happened to you during the day.

✓ If you live apart, get on the phone and make contact regularly.

✓ Be a friend to every member of your family and help others to do the same.

The problem with the world is that we draw the circle of our family too small.

Mother Theresa

CHAPTER SIXTEEN

Friendship

Let us be grateful to people who make us happy; they are the charming gardeners who make our souls blossom.

Marcel Proust

The friendships in my life, along with my family, are the most important thing to me, and every day I appreciate and am truly thankful for how special those relationships are. There is an expression that says, in order to really understand the soul of a person, look to their friends! My friends listen to me, try to understand me, tell me when I am doing something that may not add value, make me laugh and smile. The trust that has developed within each of these friendships gives me a security and a faith that I would not want to live without.

The popular definition of a friendship is that of a form of interpersonal relationship generally considered to be closer than association, although there is a range of degrees of intimacy in both friendships and associations. True friends, in my perspective, are there for the good times and the bad and love you for all your idiosyncrasies. I sent a fridge magnet to one of my friends a few weeks ago saying, "You will always be my friend; you know too much!"

According to a study documented in the June 2006 issue of the journal *American Sociological Review*, Americans are thought to be suffering a loss in the quality and quantity of close friendships since 1985. The study states that 25% of Americans have no close confidants, and the average total number of confidants per citizen has dropped from four to two.

I would question the intervention of technology in terms of the quality of friendships that we cultivate today. Facebook, although it provides an alternative form of socialising, has its pitfalls – especially as you can be "defriended" so publicly. What a bizarre way to treat people!

Friendship is something that needs to be treasured, with a great deal of value attached to it. It is not a disposable commodity purchased off the marketplace. Friendship is a great art and a great gift.

C.S. Lewis, for example, in his book *The Four Loves*, writes:

To the Ancients, Friendship seemed the happiest and most fully human of all loves; the crown of life and the school of virtue. The modern world, in comparison, ignores it. We admit of course that, besides a wife and family, a man needs a few 'friends'.

Friendship has been a very popular topic of moral philosophy, discussed by Plato, Aristotle, and the

Stoics, but less so in the modern era, until the re-emergence of contextualist and feminist approaches to ethics. In friendship, an openness to each other is found that can be seen as an enlargement of the self.

Aristotle writes that, "The excellent person is related to his friend in the same way as he is related to himself, since a friend is another self; and therefore, just as his own being is choice worthy for him, the friend's being is choice-worthy for him in the same or a similar way".

Friendship therefore opens the door to an escape from egotism or belief that the rational course of action is to pursue your own self-interest.

Research indicates that people with strong and broad social relationships are happier, healthier and live longer. Close relationships with family and friends provide love, meaning, support and increase our feelings of self-worth.

Sustaining friendship takes conscious effort. It is so important not to take for granted your friendships and showing appreciation is the key.

When you want to show appreciation to your friends for their friendship, there are a number of things you can do.

- ✓ Show gratitude for a great friendship by reciprocating acts of kindness and generosity.
- ✓ Anything you appreciate them doing, tell them and thank them and explain how it made you feel.

✓ Make mental notes about what you appreciate about each friendship; whether it is phone calls, help, invitations to dinner, etc., then do the same for them.

✓ Tell your friends how much you appreciate them. People want praise, they want to know they are appreciated, and they want to know you notice what they do for you.

✓ Every now and then, post a funny or sentimental card telling a friend how much you appreciate them.

✓ If you see an article in a paper or magazine that you think they would appreciate, cut it out and send it to them.

Something really important to remember is that when you spend time with your friend, be with them. It is a sad sign of modern times that so many people, when they are with their friends, are not really *with* them. How many times do you see people sitting with each other and spending more time on their mobile phones? So, be present Value the time you are actually with them!

What is a friend? A single soul in two bodies.

Aristotle

CHAPTER SEVENTEEN

Work to Live -
Love to Work

*Don't judge each day by the harvest
you reap, but by the seeds you plant.*

Robert Louis Stevenson

Many of us spend the biggest proportion of our lives at work and with our work colleagues – in some cases, more time than we spend at home and with our friends and relatives.

Work is fast becoming the way in which we define ourselves. It is now answering some of the traditional questions like, "Who am I?" and, "How do I find meaning and purpose?" Work is no longer just about economics; it's about identity. About fifty years ago, people had many sources of identity: religion, class, nationality, political affiliation, family roots, and geographical and cultural origins. Today, many of these, if not all, have been superseded by work.

Work is where we get to employ most of our talents. It's where we experience some of our greatest triumphs and failures. It's also the basis for our standard of living. All of this means that, when work is not working for us, we become unproductive and unfulfilled. It is really important, therefore, to make the most of what we do at work and seek to get the best out of it. Appreciating work and seeing it as a positive experience rather than a chore will certainly improve the quality of your life. A great deal of this will be down to your attitude and how you view your whole work experience.

Moreover, scientific evidence tells us that work is the best way to stay healthy, too, which is interesting. When an unemployed person with mental health problems does find work, that re-employment improves their health. And there is no evidence that people – even those who suffer from a severe mental illness – are made more ill by work. In other words, work is good for you. So whatever you do, make the most of it and enjoy it!

Here are some tips to help you to appreciate what you do and experience job satisfaction:

- ✓ Take personal responsibility for your actions and everything that you do. If you make a mistake, own up to it sooner rather than later, and always do it completely. This gets it out of the way and creates greater success, because no one has given the problem time to fester and grow.
- ✓ Be accountable for the commitments you make and, when you make a promise, keep it. Not remaining faithful to your word erodes the trust necessary for a working relationship. Once you break your word,

your team - mates will have difficulty believing that you will be there for them the next time.

✓ Share in creating a positive and emotionally comfortable working environment. This is so important. Satisfaction cannot thrive in a negative environment. If you have developed a "draining" work style, where no one tries to lift their co-workers out of the doldrums, it prevents everyone from finding emotional and even physical comfort and that will lower productivity.

✓ Make your working relationships meaningful and strive to create something meaningful and worthwhile. Everyone wants to be part of something greater than they are, whether it is contributing to the organisation, the community or the world.

✓ Keep what you do interesting and look at different ways of doing things rather than get stuck in a rut of routine that you do not enjoy. Variety is the spice of life!

✓ Greet people around you with enthusiasm and look pleased to see people, rather than just taking for granted that they are always there. This will help energise the environment and make it a friendlier place.

✓ Help each other grow and learn and actively encourage colleagues to take care of themselves by becoming more skilled and working on new projects. People who are not growing do not feel good about themselves and this will cause them to feel less important and valued. When someone feels they aren't very useful, they are not able to contribute in a positive way.

✓ Recognise your co-workers for their commitment and effort. The number one motivator for people is recognition. Saying to someone that you recognise their efforts to make your working relationship great is the best motivator you could give to them. Letting someone know that they have added value and made an important contribution is a great compliment.

✓ Make sure you recognise and celebrate your own contributions, too.

✓ Balance work and home. It is so important to get the balance right. Both are equally important in life and making sure that they complement each other is key.

Understanding the need for feeling satisfied and contributing to that necessity in your work life will make you happy. These tips will help you maintain a fulfilling relationship with your work and help you to appreciate what you do and get ultimate job satisfaction.

*The best preparation for good work
tomorrow is to do good work today.*

Elbert Hubbard

Chapter Eighteen

Lifelong Learning

It's what you learn after you know it all that counts.

Harry S Truman

We learn something new every day, and that is one of the joys of being alive. It is a fascinating and evolving world that we live in and everywhere around you there are new things to sense and experience.

Since Victorian times, people have believed that education is good for you, that it has the effect of cod-liver oil: taken in regular doses, it makes you into a better, healthier individual. There are numerous benefits to learning, which include the following and can help make the country into an improved and more prosperous place:

- ✓ Increases self-confidence and self-awareness
- ✓ Offers you ways to something new and keep your life fresh and interesting
- ✓ You can save money as you learn to "do it yourself"
- ✓ Gives you a feeling of confidence and self-worth through accomplishment
- ✓ Keeps your mind sharp and active, which is a good investment as you get older

✓ Improves memory and recall of positive experiences
✓ Great for meeting new people who share your interests
✓ Offers you an opportunity to learn a new skill for work and increase your income
✓ Gives you a new interest that you can share with family and friends
✓ Gives us purpose and interest in life

The ability to learn and to actively do something with what you have learnt is such an important ability. We can easily amass a great deal of knowledge and information; however, if we don't do something positive with it, then, in some respects, it could be considered a bit of a waste of time! There are many health benefits to learning and evidence shows the importance of keeping our brain as a goal-seeking mechanism; active, interested and receptive.

It is also useful to understand that we are all different and we will learn in different ways. Knowing and understanding your learning style can make a big difference to how well you learn and at what speed. There are so many interesting models about learning. Here are a few types:

Auditory or Visual Learners – This indicates the sensory mode you prefer when processing information. Auditory learners tend to learn more effectively through listening, while visual learners process information by seeing it in print or other visual modes, including film, pictures, diagrams or videos when available.

Applied or Conceptual Learners – This describes the types of learning tasks and learning situations you prefer and find most easy to handle. If you are an applied learner, you prefer tasks that involve real objects and situations. Practical, real-life learning situations are ideal for you. If you are a conceptual learner, you prefer to work with language and ideas; practical applications are not necessary for understanding.

Spatial or Non-spatial Learners – This reveals your ability to work with spatial relationships. Spatial learners are able to visualise or "mentally see" how things work or how they are positioned in space. Their strengths may include drawing, assembling things, or repairing. Non-spatial learners lack skills in positioning things in space. Instead, they tend to rely on verbal or language skills.

Social or Independent Learners – This reveals your preferred level of interaction with other people in the learning process. If you are a social learner, you prefer to work with others – both peers and instructors – closely and directly. You tend to be people-oriented and enjoy personal interaction. If you are an independent learner, you prefer to work and study alone. You tend to be self-directed or self-motivated, and often goal-oriented.

Creative or Pragmatic Learners – This describes the approach you prefer to take toward learning tasks. Creative learners are imaginative and innovative. They prefer to learn through discovery or experimentation. They are comfortable taking risks and following hunches. Pragmatic learners are practical, logical, and systematic. They seek order and are comfortable following rules.

In order to learn really well, it is also important for you to look after your brain. Here are a few useful tips to help you:

- ✓ **Mental stimulation exercises** – Learning new information and skills across your entire lifespan helps to keep your brain strong even in the later years of life. Activities that have the highest value for brain health are those that are novel and complex to each particular person.
- ✓ **Exercise regularly** – Exercise has the positive effect of enhancing successful ageing. Exercise performed on a routine basis may not only reduce the risk of neurodegenerative disease, but also may help to slow the course of an existing disease, such as Alzheimer's.
- ✓ **Socialise and have fun!** – Friends provide opportunities to enable the sharing of experiences, new learning, challenges, emotions, trust, and understanding. Friendship also provides the necessary motivation towards activity and involvement and increases the desire to learn.
- ✓ **Slow down and appreciate the silence** – Our society is evolving at an increasing rate, leaving us with little time to relax and process our environment. Our brains require time to process information more deeply, in order to gain more benefit from our daily experiences.
- ✓ **Adopt a nutrient-rich diet** – Over-consumption of high calorie food is a major issue for modern society.

Understanding why we eat and what we eat is one of the most critical influences on our health and longevity. Brain health-promoting nutrients include the Omega-3 fatty acids found in foods such as fish, flax seed, and nuts.

✓ **Maintain strong connections** – Our ability to communicate and interact with others is critical to maintaining strong connections. Isolation has been shown to reduce our overall health. Research demonstrates the importance of a social network in reducing the risk of dementia.

Learning can be huge fun, enlightening, stimulating, fulfilling and has so many health benefits. Life offers you so much and it is up to you to open your eyes to look up and around and seek out those opportunities to learn and grow. How exciting is that?

Anyone who stops learning is old,
whether at twenty or eighty.

Henry Ford

Chapter Nineteen

Probortunities

Problems are to the mind what exercise is to the muscles – they toughen and make strong.

Norman Vincent Peale

"In the middle of difficulty," observed Albert Einstein, "lies opportunity." The words of a genius, indeed. Every dark cloud has a silver lining, and being grateful for our situation, even if we don't like everything about it, allows us to be thankful for the opportunity to learn something new.

There is a great word, which I use often: "probortunity". This is the hybrid word that helps you to view all problems as opportunities.

There are times, of course, where this can be really challenging – but it's so much better to seek out the solution than to give up and get trapped in an emotional cul-de-sac feeling fed up and negative!

We are all faced with challenges every day of our lives – problems to solve and hurdles to overcome. It's one of the things that makes life interesting. So much of the way you approach problems is around your mind-set because, if you can change your perspective and view problems as probortunities, then you will find a whole new world opens up to you.

There is an expression when you don't like something that you can shut up, put up or get out. There is another approach, however, and that is to change your attitude. Once you do this, you will go from feeling like the whole world is against you to feeling like a solution is just around the corner.

Once you start to believe that you have opportunities all around you, change really begins to happen in your life. If you are regularly looking for solutions to your problems, you will actually begin to attract opportunities to you. The opportunities will appear as a result of your expectation of them.

This is all part of using your mind to change how you see your problems. When you see everything as an opportunity, instead of a problem, your focus begins to shift. Before you know it, you will begin to experience real, lasting changes that will have a powerful effect on your life.

Too often, we focus on problems and fail to see that there are numerous opportunities right in front of us.

When you focus on your problems, when you only think of your problems, when you only think of what is wrong in your life, you will only see problems.

Think of what it is you really need to resolve and then think about how you can accomplish your goal. You may not find immediate answers, but along the way, when you accept that you will find a solution, you begin to experience a shift. You will go from feeling like you can't do anything to starting to believe that maybe you just might be able to find a solution.

If you're out of work, look at this as an opportunity to now do anything that you want: to get the right job, start a business, relocate. You may be heartbroken about a relationship that has finished. However, it may be releasing you to meet someone far better, with whom you will be happier. Whatever the situation, it is important to look at the door that has just opened, rather than focusing on the one that has shut.

Tips to Turn Problems into Opportunities

Use positive vocabulary – Even if you have to convey a negative thought or emotion, say it in a positive way. Think about the kind of language you use in your own mind and out loud with others. Address negative words and turn them into positives. Take the "t" out of can't.

Reconsider obstacles – Try to view problems as something you can work through, instead of obstacles that prevent you from getting what you want. Seek out another way. There is *always* another way.

Force yourself to smile – Release some tension and project some positive energy by smiling at someone or telling a joke. It will take the tension out of the situation, if only a little.

Focus on things you're good at – When you are dealing with challenging situations, you need to feel strong and confident. A little bit of boosting your self-esteem will go a long way. Thinking about your strengths will help to boost confidence, which will help you to deal better with things.

Ask for help – There is nothing weak about asking for help and no man is an island. Reap the benefits of talking about your problems. Friends and family can also give you another perspective on your problem that will help you get through the tough times. A problem shared in a constructive way is a problem halved for sure.

Sleep on it – Before you go to bed at night, if you have some problems to deal with, take a sheet of paper and draw a line down the middle. Write down all your problems on the left hand side and then think of the opportunity on the other. Sleep on it and you will be amazed how much better you feel in the morning. I do this often and find my dreams have a great way of untangling and creating another perspective.

Reduce stress – Try to reduce your stress level by doing one positive thing each day, by giving yourself a little more free time, going to bed early, or visiting friends or anything that helps. You will not be able to deal with problems as effectively if you are highly strung or agitated. A clear head will help you to make better decisions.

Make a plan – Sometimes it is useful to gauge your reaction to problems by asking yourself how important and relevant they are to your life. Ask yourself whether this problem will still be a major issue in 3 weeks, 6 months, or one year.

Learn – With every problem, recognise and focus on what you have learnt – really stop and consider the lessons and how they will positively impact on your life in the future.

Say thank you – This may sound a bit bonkers to some; however, one thing I have learnt to do is to say thank you to my problems, because each one has made me a little wiser, a little stronger, and created some amazing probortunities!

When it is dark enough, you can see the stars.

Ralph Waldo Emerson

CHAPTER TWENTY

The World Around You

*Nature does not hurry, yet
everything is accomplished.*

Lao Tzu

In the fast paced world in which we now live ,it seems that we take so much for granted and miss so much of the beauty that is around us. Whilst I was finishing this book, I went down to stay in Dartmouth. It really is one of the most beautiful places that I have ever been and I stayed in a beautiful converted boathouse overlooking the river Dart. Getting up at five every morning to watch the sun rise and going on long walks through woods and along coastal paths, I appreciated every second I was there.

Walking back along the harbour side one day, I noticed a group of schoolchildren, all of them with hand-held gadgets, deep in concentration, seemingly oblivious to the beauty that surrounded them and each other, for that matter. This is something I notice so often on my travels. Technology seems to have taken a grip and the present world around is barely acknowledged.

Taking notice is so important and the key to taking notice is mindfulness, a subject I have already addressed in Chapter Nine. However, as it is such an important factor with regards to the art of appreciation it will be good to explore it in a little bit more detail. Mindfulness is often defined as "the state of being attentive to and aware of what is taking place in the present". Two key elements of mindfulness are to make it intentional and accept without judgement what we notice.

In other words, mindfulness is "openly experiencing what is there". It is about having a full awareness of what is around us using all our senses. It is about observing all this but not getting caught up in thinking and worrying about what we are observing. It then gives us more control of what we decide to give our attention. A growing number of scientific studies are showing the benefits of mindfulness in many aspects of our lives, including our physical and mental well-being, our relationships and our performance at school and at work. It appears to have benefits for everyone, from children through to the elderly.

It is not really something that we do naturally, so it takes lots of practice.

One key area of mindfulness relates to your interaction with others. When you find yourself wanting to prematurely end a conversation, examine what it is about the exchange that is causing you to want to move on. Are you anxious to find a "better", more exciting conversation partner? Are you thinking about something else? Instead, make an effort to fully listen. Give yourself permission to be truly present with that person and then react attentively and honestly to what they are actually saying. It will help you to become a better listener, knowing yourself better and building patience.

It is also important to become aware of the judgements you automatically form when you meet someone for the first time. Do you immediately start to assign attributes to them and create your own mental storyline about them according to whether you initially like or don't like them? Try to be aware of your reactions. We can be very quick to judge and often we can short-change people without taking time to see through the superficial first encounter.

If you suspend opinions before you get to know someone, you're open to the opportunity of seeing that person for who he or she really is.

Another good time to be mindful is when you are eating. Many of us eat unconsciously, shovelling food into our mouths, rarely tasting much beyond the first bite. Instead, eat slowly, tasting each bite, and savouring the texture and flavour. Chew slowly, thinking about how the food got to the table, and appreciating how it fuels your body. The same goes for liquid (alcoholic or non-alcoholic). Sip it.

The more aware you are about how and what you eat, the healthier your food choices become and the more relaxing and enjoyable mealtimes will be.

During your leisure time, connect with the timeless rhythms of nature. Whether you are gardening, biking, hiking or strolling, all these things put you in harmony with the natural environment. It is such a glorious world out there with so much to see and sensory experiences to embrace and enjoy.

The goal of mindfulness is to be fully present. It's easier to achieve this state when you're in a natural setting. Being outdoors takes you away from the ticking of the clock, the ringing of the telephone and all the distractions of modern life that fragment our attention.

One great tip is to slow down and practise the "philosophy of slow". Doing something slowly diminishes your stress level, builds patience, helps us appreciate things that don't offer "immediate gratification", and often produces better, more satisfying results.

Being present in each moment, one can, in the world we find ourselves living in, feel that we are conditioned to review our past and plan our future. If you want the future to be different, the only place that you can stand and work with it is in the here and now. Noticing the world, right here and right now, is a great place to start really appreciating the wonders of the world that you have around you.

We do not inherit the earth from our ancestors,
we borrow it from our children.

Native American Proverb

Chapter Twenty-One

Sensing Your World

*The senses do not deceive us,
but the judgment does.*

Johann Wolfgang Von Goethe

The way in which we appreciate life is through our senses. They are ultimately our connection to everything that surrounds us. They are the sum and substance of all our individual and shared experiences. They are necessary to our survival and they are also tools to be utilised to enhance our appreciation of pretty much everything.

Part of how we appreciate is by paying attention to our sensory experiences. This can be through what we see, what we hear, our feelings, what we touch, taste and smell.

Are you fully engaging and using all the gifts that you have?

Traditionally, there are five senses: sight, smell, taste, touch, and hearing. As far back as the 1760s, the famous philosopher Immanuel Kant proposed that our knowledge of the outside world depended on our modes of perception. In order to define what is "extrasensory", we need to define what is "sensory". Each of the five senses consists of organs with specialised cells that have receptors for specific stimuli. These cells have links to the nervous system and to the brain.

Sensing is done at primitive levels in the cells and integrated into sensations in the nervous system. Sight is probably the most developed sense in humans, followed closely by hearing.

We live in such a fast-paced world that we can so easily diminish the value of perceiving all that our senses have to offer. We need to notice things to appreciate them! This is sometimes easier said than done. We consciously register only a small percentage of what we perceive. We learn to filter using our Reticular Activating System and we decide what is important and disregard the rest. To build appreciation it is critical to adjust our filters so we perceive more.

Acknowledging and celebrating your senses is a great place to start. Practise appreciating variation, beauty, novelty, colour, pattern, rhythm, tone, sensations, flavours, scents, and feelings that your world offers you. Appreciation is opening up your perceptions. Noticing any sensory experience requires attention and awareness. Consciously ask yourself questions about your experiences.

Understanding your senses is a great place to start. Here is a brief overview of the five basic senses:

Sight

Sight or vision is the ability of the eyes to focus and detect images of visible light on photoreceptors in the retina of each eye that generates electrical nerve impulses for varying colours, hues, and brightness.

The retina is covered with two basic types of light-sensitive cells: rods and cones. The cone cells are sensitive to colour and are located in the part of the retina called the fovea, where the light is focused by the lens.

The rod cells are not sensitive to colour, but have greater sensitivity to light than the cone cells. These cells are located around the fovea and are responsible for peripheral vision and night vision. The eye is connected to the brain through the optic nerve. The point of this connection is called the "blind spot" because it is insensitive to light. Experiments have shown that the back of the brain maps the visual input from the eyes.

Hearing

The ear is the organ of hearing. The outer ear protrudes away from the head and is shaped like a cup to direct sounds toward the tympanic membrane, which transmits vibrations to the inner ear through a series of small bones in the middle ear called the *malleus*, *incus* and *stapes*.

The inner ear, or cochlea, is a spiral-shaped chamber covered internally by nerve fibres that react to the vibrations and transmit impulses to the brain via the auditory nerve.

The brain combines the input of our two ears to determine the direction and distance of sounds. The human ear can perceive frequencies from 16 cycles per second, which is a very deep bass, to 28,000 cycles per second, which is a very high pitch. Bats and dolphins can detect frequencies higher than 100,000 cycles per second.

Taste

The receptors for taste, called taste buds, are situated chiefly in the tongue, but they are also located in the roof of the mouth and near the pharynx. They are able to detect four basic tastes: salty, sweet, bitter, and sour.

Generally, the taste buds close to the tip of the tongue are sensitive to sweet tastes, whereas those in the back of the tongue are sensitive to bitter tastes. The tongue also can detect a sensation known as "umami" – a pleasant, savoury taste – from taste receptors sensitive to amino acids. The taste buds on top and on the side of the tongue are sensitive to salty and sour tastes.

At the base of each taste bud is a nerve that sends the sensations to the brain. The sense of taste functions in co-ordination with the sense of smell. The number of taste buds varies substantially from individual to individual, but greater numbers increase sensitivity. Women generally have a greater number of taste buds than men.

Smell

The nose is the organ responsible for the sense of smell. The cavity of the nose is lined with mucous membranes that have smell receptors connected to the olfactory nerve. The smells themselves consist of vapours of various substances. The smell receptors interact with the molecules of these vapours and transmit the sensations to the brain.

The nose also has a structure called the vomeronasal organ, whose function has not been determined, but which is suspected of being sensitive to pheromones that influence the reproductive cycle. The smell receptors are sensitive to seven types of sensations that can be characterised as camphor, musk, flower, mint, ether, acrid or putrid. The sense of smell is sometimes temporarily lost when a person has a cold. Dogs have a sense of smell that is many times more sensitive than that of humans.

Remember that the way that you experience the world is predominantly down to your senses, so, by consciously appreciating and filtering what you perceive, you will become more in control of engaging the kind of experiences that you enjoy.

Perception is a gift. Appreciation is an attitude and a way of being.

Nothing can cure the soul but the senses, just as nothing can cure the senses but the soul.

Oscar Wilde

CHAPTER TWENTY-TWO

Sweet Dreams

*Early to bed and early to rise makes
a man healthy, wealthy, and wise.*

Benjamin Franklin

One thing that we maybe don't appreciate enough is our sleep and the importance of our sleep. I suppose, because we are not consciously around for most of it, we take for granted the wonderful healing properties that sleep provides. I went on a sleep course a few years ago and found it fascinating.

I learnt that the benefits of sleep impact nearly every area of daily life. While it may be obvious that sleep is beneficial, most people don't realise how much sleep they need and why it is so important.

According to the Division of Sleep Medicine at Harvard Medical School, your body manages and requires sleep in the same way that it regulates the need for eating, drinking and breathing. Extensive research has been done on the effects of sleep. These studies have consistently shown that sleep plays a vital role in promoting physical health, longevity, and emotional well-being. I have to say that if I don't sleep well, I feel quite tearful and sensitive.

There are so many benefits that sleep promotes. First of all it helps to repair your body and produces extra protein molecules while you're sleeping that help strengthen your ability to fight infection and stay healthy. These molecules help your immune system to mend your body at a cellular level when you are stressed or have been exposed to compromising elements such as pollutants and infectious bacteria.

Your cardiovascular system is constantly under pressure and sleep helps to reduce the levels of stress and inflammation in your body. High levels of "inflammatory markers" are linked to heart disease and strokes. Sleep can also help keep blood pressure and cholesterol levels (which play a role in heart disease) in check. A good night's sleep can help lower blood pressure and elevated levels of stress hormones, which are a natural result of today's fast-paced lifestyle.

High blood pressure can be life-threatening, and the physical effects of stress can produce wear and tear on your body and degenerate cells, which propels the ageing process. Sleep helps to slow these effects and encourages a state of relaxation.

That "foggy" feeling that you struggle with when deprived of sleep makes it difficult to concentrate. This often leads to memory problems with facts, faces, lessons, or even conversations. Sleeping well eliminates these difficulties because, as you sleep, your brain is busy organising and correlating memories.

One of the great benefits of sleep is that it allows your brain to better process new experiences and knowledge, increasing your understanding and retention. So the next time you hear someone say, "why don't you sleep on it?" take their advice.

Sleep helps to regulate the hormones that affect and control your appetite. Studies have shown that when your body is deprived of sleep, the normal hormone balances are interrupted and your appetite increases. Unfortunately, this increase in appetite doesn't lead to a craving for fruits and veggies. Rather, your body longs for foods high in calories, fats, and carbohydrates.

If you're trying to lose those stubborn few pounds that just keep hanging around, consider the benefits of sleep on weight-control and make sure that you are getting enough sleep each day.

Researchers have shown that lack of sleep may lead to Type 2 diabetes by affecting how your body processes glucose, which is the carbohydrate your cells use for fuel.

The Division of Sleep Medicine at Harvard Medical School reports that a study showed a healthy group of people who had reduced their sleep from eight to four hours per night processed glucose more slowly. Other research initiatives have revealed that adults who usually sleep less than five hours per night have a greatly increased risk of developing diabetes.

With insufficient sleep during the night, many people become agitated or moody the following day. When limited sleep becomes a chronic issue, studies have shown it can lead to long-term mood disorders such as depression or anxiety.

By appreciating the benefits of sleep, you can make a difference in your quality of life, as well as the length of your life.

Tips to help you sleep well:

✓ Go to bed when you feel tired and stick to a routine of getting up at the same time every day, whether you still feel tired or not.

✓ Stop drinking tea or coffee by mid-afternoon. If you want a hot drink in the evening, try something milky or herbal.

✓ Avoid a lot of alcohol. It may help you fall asleep, but you will almost certainly wake up during the night.

✓ Avoid eating or drinking a lot late at night.

✓ If you've had a bad night, don't sleep in the next day – it will make it harder to get off to sleep the following night.

✓ Make sure that your bed and bedroom are comfortable – not too hot, not too cold, not too noisy.

✓ Make sure that your mattress supports you properly. If it's too firm, your hips and shoulders are under pressure. If it's too soft, your body sags which is bad for your back.

✓ Replace your mattress every 10 years to get the best support and comfort.

- ✓ Get some exercise every day – the recommended amount is 30 minutes a day.
- ✓ Take some time to relax properly before going to bed.
- ✓ Take a hot bath with relaxing oils or bubble bath.
- ✓ If something is troubling you and there is nothing you can do about it right away, try writing it down before going to bed and all the potential opportunities that can arise from it.

A well-spent day brings happy sleep.

Leonardo da Vinci

CHAPTER TWENTY-THREE

Manners Maketh Man ... and Woman!

Treat everyone with politeness, even those who are rude to you - not because they are nice, but because you are.

Author Unknown

One of the things I appreciate most of all about people is good manners; this is such an attractive quality and demonstrates respect and consideration for others. I hear so many people these days lament the lack of good manners in today's society and sadly, I have to say I agree. There does tend to be a "me first" attitude that can manifest itself in rudeness and selfishness.

We learn the importance of saying "thank you" as little children. We are taught that habit because it is "good manners". This childhood lesson is extremely powerful and goes a long way to making other people feel good and appreciated. No one likes to feel that they are not being considered or taken for granted.

Good manners, historically, are a set of behaviours that identify someone as being civilised and cultured.

Manners are usually taught from a very young age, with some people receiving additional training in etiquette, formal rules of conduct which apply to a variety of situations.

The precise behaviours involved in good manners will vary from place to place. Cultural traditions play an important role in manners, as do religious beliefs, social status, and economic class. What may be good manners in one culture may vary quite a bit. As a general rule, people learn the manners that pertain to their particular social, economic, and cultural situation, and travellers ideally learn the specific rules of conduct needed to fit in as they visit other societies.

Having travelled fairly extensively across different cultures, it is interesting to see how much they can vary. However, from my personal observation, whilst the precise nature of manners may vary, the underlying principles do not. Good manners involve treating people with respect and courtesy, and in making sure that other people feel comfortable in a variety of situations. The old Biblical rule of "do as you would be done by" is sometimes used as an illustration of how manners are supposed to work.

It seems that, generally, people with good manners are more likely to get ahead in the world of business, and they also find themselves more commonly invited as guests and welcomed in society. In tense social situations, an awareness of good manners and social rules of behaviour can help to diffuse tension, or at least to avoid a serious incident, and someone's attention to proper codes of conduct will be remembered. People who travel and take the time to learn about the codes of conduct in regions they are visiting will often find their way smoothed, and they will be welcomed back in the future.

So a good set of manners is a very useful set of behaviours and will most certainly help people around you to feel respected and appreciated.

Tips on good manners

- ✓ If you are in a mixed group, always greet the elders and the women first.
- ✓ Try not to shout to be heard.
- ✓ Try not to interrupt others while they're talking.
- ✓ Stand up when an elder or a guest enters the room and try not to sit until you've offered them a seat.
- ✓ Offer a glass of water (and preferably a cup of tea) to anyone who steps into your home/office.
- ✓ Try not to continue to watch TV or surf the net when you have a visitor.
- ✓ Lower the music or TV volume when others are talking or trying to sleep.
- ✓ Try not to ask too many intimate or invasive questions the first few times that you meet a person.
- ✓ Try not to comment on personal appearances or clothes in a negative way; if you cannot say something complimentary, Try not to say anything at all.
- ✓ Wash your hands before and after a meal.
- ✓ Ask for whatever you want instead of reaching out directly or pointing at dishes.

✓ Try not to talk with food in your mouth.
✓ Wait until everyone else is sitting down before starting to eat.
✓ Help clear the dishes.
✓ Try not to read while eating.
✓ Try not to talk on your mobile phone during the meal and, if you must get up in-between, ask to be excused.
✓ Write thank you cards.
✓ Hold doors open.
✓ Help people with putting coats on and taking them off.
✓ If you see someone struggling, help them.

A man's manners are a mirror in which he shows his portrait.

Johann Wolfgang von Goethe

CHAPTER TWENTY-FOUR

Living in a Material World

*If everyone demanded peace instead of another
television set, then there'd be peace.*

John Lennon

There's an old adage that says, "it's more important
to want what you have than to have what you want."
I think that is a great phrase, and think of it when
I observe people experience stress over *not* having
what they want or what they think they want!

Surveys in Britain and the U.S. show that people are no
happier now than they were in the 1950s – despite
massive economic growth. We own more cars, more
homes, eat out more often and enjoy endless other
commodities that weren't around then, such as big-
screen TVs, microwave ovens, mobile phones and
other handheld wireless devices.

Psychologist Dr David G. Myers, author of *The
American Paradox: Spiritual Hunger in an Age of Plenty*
believes through his research that, compared with
their grandparents, today's young adults have grown
up with much more affluence, slightly less happiness
and a much greater risk of depression.

The indication is that, despite all the material possessions we now own, it doesn't necessarily make us any happier. Personally, I really struggle with consumerism and the way that we are encouraged to become more materialistic.

So much advertising is geared up to make people feel inadequate and shamelessly encourages people to dip into their depleting bank accounts or to live beyond their means. I would go as far to say that we are becoming so greedy that we hardly have time to appreciate what we have before we are off in pursuit of the next thing! It seems to be so much about quick fix solutions and instant gratification.

Some of the trips I have taken to Ethiopia in the last few years have highlighted to me the rather vulgar and sickening wastage we tolerate in western society. At least a third of the food we buy, we throw away. So many of the possessions we have are not considered treasures, as they would be in poorer societies, and most of what we have is considered disposable.

Sadly, in the materialist world where only money and beauty matter, many people seem to care only about what other people think about them, while trying to be what they think other people want them to be. Trying to be better than each other, they compete with fashion, cars and gadgets and are perfect fodder for the booming cosmetic industry.

Without the guidance of any believable moral authority, the younger generation now look to actors, pop stars, sporting heroes and even reality TV stars as their role models, benchmarking themselves against false images and hyped media tales. Dangerously, they take their values from fashionable pop culture trends, and they live their lives learning mostly from their mistakes.

Let's face it: some of these so-called icons are not the best role models, and very often they fall from their pedestal rather disgracefully, leaving individuals unhappy when the world fails to provide them with anything worth believing in. They often become cynical, suspicious of authority, rebellious, angry at life, and sometimes even self-destructive.

Psychologists' research is rife with regard to the possible effects of this consumer culture on people's mental well-being. As with all things psychological, the relationship between mental state and materialism is complex: indeed, researchers are still trying to ascertain whether materialism stokes unhappiness or unhappiness fuels materialism, or both.

Given that we are all exposed to the same consumerist culture, it's interesting that some people develop stronger materialistic values than others. A line of research suggests that insecurity lies at the heart of consumerist cravings. Indeed, it's not money per se, but the striving for it, that's linked to unhappiness.

It is, however, important to put things in perspective, because it would be unreasonable to condemn material things entirely. It is more about addressing the role and status they are accorded in your life and challenging the value and importance that you place upon them. The key is to find a balance: to appreciate what you have, but not at the expense of the things that really matter – your family, community and spirituality.

On balance, feeding your soul as well as your bank account seems well worth consideration! On that note, let me share a great story about a Mexican fisherman with you.

Once upon a time there was an investment banker who was on holiday with his family in Mexico. They decided to take a trip to a small coastal village for a change of scenery from the big tourist resort that they were staying in. Whilst the banker was standing with his son on the pier admiring the view, a small boat with just one fisherman docked alongside them.

Inside the small boat were several large yellow-fin tuna. The investment banker complimented the Mexican on the quality of his fish and asked how long it took to catch them.

The Mexican replied, "Only a little while."

The banker then asked why he didn't stay out longer and catch more fish.

The Mexican said he had enough to support his family's immediate needs.

The banker then asked, "But what do you do with the rest of your time?"

The Mexican fisherman said, "I sleep late, fish a little, play with my children, take a siesta with my wife, Maria, and stroll into the village each evening, where I sip wine and play my guitar with my amigos. I have a full and busy life."

The banker scoffed, "I am a Harvard MBA and could help you. You should spend more time fishing and with the proceeds, buy a bigger boat. With the proceeds from the bigger boat, you could buy more boats.Eventually, you would have a fleet of fishing boats.

"You would of course need to leave this small coastal fishing village and move to Mexico City, then to Los Angeles and eventually New York, where you will be able to run your expanding enterprise."

The Mexican fisherman looked at him and asked, "But, how long will this all take?"

To which the banker replied, "About 15 years."

"But what will I do then?" asked the fisherman

The banker laughed and said, "Well, that's the great part. When the time is right, you would sell your company stock to the public and become very rich. You would make millions, and then you will be able to retire."

"So after I make these millions and retire, what will I do?" asked the fisherman.

The banker smiled and said, "Then you can move to a small coastal fishing village where you would sleep late, fish a little, play with your grandchildren, take a siesta with your wife, and stroll to the village in the evenings where you could sip wine and play your guitar with your amigos. How good does that sound?"

To which the Mexican fisherman smiled back at the banker and said nothing.

It is useless to shout to the drowning moneylender, "Give me your hand!" He does not know how to give. Instead, shout: "Take my hand!" and he will clutch at it.

Author Unknown

CHAPTER TWENTY-FIVE

What are YOU for?

The purpose of life is a life of purpose.

Robert Byrne

When my friend Melanie's son Matthew was little, he used to go around asking people, "What are you for?"

What a great question!

I wonder how often we stop and ask ourselves the same question?

According to some philosophies, our purpose is the central key to living a positive human life. Others believe that our purpose is not fixed and instead we can freely choose what we want it to be. It is, indeed, a deeply philosophical and never-ending debate. For some people, a purpose in life is an essential and fundamental aim, and for other people, fulfilment and purpose is halted by fear of failure or lack of motivation.

Modern spiritual philosophy sees the purpose in life as improving the environment and the world generally. In the most immediate sense, this can mean that each individual identifies the special talents they possess and uses them as a gift to serve others. I have been reading recently about the Life-Purpose System, a concept originally formulated by Dan Millman in his book *The Life You Were Born to Live* – well worth a read.

It would appear that people who have meaning and purpose in their lives are happier, feel more in control and get more out of everything they do. They also experience less stress, anxiety and depression.

But where do we find "meaning and purpose "in our lives? Perhaps it is from our religious faith, our friends, our family, our partner, a hobby or doing a job that makes a difference. The answers will vary for each of us, as we are unique.

The Dalai Lama, for example, believes that the purpose of life is the pursuit of happiness. One important distinction to make is that statistically, those people who behave or appear to be happy tend to be more altruistic and less egotistic.

According to the hierarchy of needs outlined by psychologist Abraham Maslow, belongingness and usefulness to others are fundamental to meeting human needs and conducive to building happiness.

Personally, I like the concept that we are all connected and that if we hurt others, we will only end up hurting ourselves, so we have a purpose to be kind and considerate in our behaviour towards others. By taking more personal responsibility for the consequences of our actions, our purpose becomes more honourable.

If we approach every life situation with positive and kind intentions, then we will be making our own great individual contribution to creating a better world.

The understanding that we hold in our hands the power to inspire others, change a life, a mind, or a circumstance today is a powerful insight and motivator and something to be truly appreciative of.

However small or great our actions, whatever our purpose is, we have the power to make a difference in everything we do and this story sums this up so well.

The Starfish Story

One day a man was walking along the beach when he noticed a small boy picking something up and gently throwing it into the ocean. Approaching the boy, he asked, "What are you doing?"

The little boy replied, "I am saving all the starfish that have been stranded on the beach. The surf is up and the tide is going out and if I don't throw them back, they will die".

The man looked around and noticed that there were miles and miles of beach and literally thousands of starfish.

He looked at the beach again and then at the small boy and said, "Well, you won't make much of a difference, will you?"

After listening politely, the little boy bent down, picked up another starfish, and threw it back into the sea. Then, looking up, he smiled and said to the man,"I made a difference for that one."

Be the change you want to see in the world.

Mahatma Gandhi

Your Gratitude Plan

Now that you have read all about gratitude and the benefits of adopting an attitude of gratitude, it is up to you to decide what you are going to do. Making gratitude a daily habit is really important.

Here are some useful steps to follow to help you to do this:

✓ **Make a personal commitment**
The effects of gratitude gain momentum over time and with practice.

✓ **Make a start**
Sit down with pen and paper or at your computer and start making a list of all the things you are grateful for.

✓ **Write it down**
This is really important so that it is visible and tangible.

✓ **Feel it**
Really tap into your senses and emotions no matter what is going on around you.

✓ **Choose a set time in the day**
This is the best way to sustain a habit.

✓ **Practise present moment gratitude**
Throughout the day get into the habit of stopping and focusing on things that you are grateful for.

✓ **Share the gratitude**
It is a good idea to partner with someone and get into the habit of sharing things you are grateful for with each other.

✓ **Do highlights**
At the end of every day think about the best three things that have happened to you. Share these if you can.

✓ **Keep a gratitude journal**
At the end of this book there is a 28 day gratitude journal for you to write your 3 highlights down and to keep a log of all the things that you appreciate daily.

✓ **Stick with it**
It takes 21- 28 days to form a new habit.

✓ **Allow yourself to be human**
If you miss the odd day here and there just pick up where you left off. Sometimes if you are having a bit of a bad time it can be challenging to think of things to be grateful for. However, if you search you will find something. Below is a list of a few things to be appreciative for to get you started:

People

Parents - For giving you the opportunity to be alive in the first place.
Family - For being your closest kin in the world.
Friends - For being your companions in life.
Enemies - For helping you uncover your blind spots so you can become a better person.
Strangers - For brightening up your days when you least expect it.
Teachers - For their dedication and for passing on knowledge to you.

Yourself

Your speech - For giving you the outlet to express yourself.
Your heart - For pumping blood to all the parts of your body
Your immune system - For fighting the germs that enter your body.
Your hands - So you can touch and feel things.
Your legs - For helping you to move about.
Your mind - For the ability to think, to store memories and to create new solutions.
Your good health - For enabling you to do what you want to do.

Emotions

Tears - For helping you express your deepest emotions.
Disappointment - So you know the things that matter to you most.
Fears -So you know your opportunities for growth.
Pain - For you to become a stronger person.

Sadness - For you to appreciate the spectrum of human emotions.

Happiness - For you to soak in and appreciate the beauty of life.

Your Senses

Sight - For letting you see the colours of life.

Hearing - For letting you hear the orchestra and the soundtrack of your life.

Touch - For letting you feel the texture of life.

Smell - For letting you smell the scented world we live in.

Taste - For letting you savour the sweetness and spice of life.

Nature

The Sun - For bringing us light and enabling life .

Sunset - For a beautiful way to end the day.

Moon and Stars - For brightening up our night sky.

Sunrise - For a beautiful way to start the day.

Rain - For washing and cleansing the world.

Snow - For making winter even more beautiful.

Rainbows - For a beautiful sight to look forward to after rain.

Oxygen - For making our life possible.

The Earth - For creating the environment for life to begin.

Mother Nature - For covering our world in beauty.

Life

Time - For a system to organise yourself and keep track of activities.

Your job - For giving you a source of living and purpose.
Your mistakes - For helping you to improve and become better.
Pain - For helping you to mature and become stronger.
Laughter - For serenading your life with joy.
Love - For letting you feel what it means to truly be alive.
Life's challenges - For helping you grow and become who you are.
Life - For giving you the chance to experience all that you're experiencing and will experience in time to come.

Thank you

We have been using the word "Thank you" for well over 1500 years. It comes from the same origin as the German word "danke" and both ultimately come from the proto-germanic 'thankojan'. Historians believe that the word "Thank" is actually related to the word "Think".

In whichever language you say it; it is a conversational expression of gratitude. Here are a few ways in other languages to pronounce it:

Language	Thank you	Pronunciation
Afrikaans	dankie	*dahn*-kee
Arabic	shukran	shoe-krahn
Chinese, Cantonese	do jeh	daw-dyeh
Chinese, Mandarin	xie xie	syeh-syeh
Czech	dêkuji	*deh*-ku-yih
Danish	tak	tahg
Finnish	kiitos	*kee*-toas
French	merci	mehr-*see*
German	danke	*dahn*-kah
Greek	efharisto	ef-har-rih-*stowe*
Hebrew	toda	toh-*dah*

Language	Thank you	Pronunciation
Hindi, Hindustani	sukria	shoo-kree-a
Indonesian/ Malayan	terima kasih	t'ree-ma kas-seh
Italian	grazie	*gra*-see
Japanese	arigato	ahree- gah-tow
Korean	kamsa hamnida	kahm-sah=ham- nee-da
Norwegian	takk	tahk
Philippines (Tagalog)	salamat po	sah-*lah*-maht poh
Polish	dziekuje	dsyen-koo-yeh
Portuguese	obrigado	oh-bree-*gah*-doh
Russian	spasibo	spah-*see*-boh
Spanish	gracias	*gra*-see-us
Sri Lanka (Sinhak)	istutiy	isst-too-tee
Swahili	asante	ah-*sahn*-teh
Swedish	tack	tahkk
Thai	kawp-kun krap/ka'	kowpkoom- krahp/khak
Turkish	tesekkür ederim	teh-sheh-kur=eh- deh-rim

Inspirational Quotes

I love inspirational quotes and have used them throughout the book. Here is a selection of others for you to read through to inspire and motivate you.

Happiness cannot be travelled to, owned, earned, worn or consumed. Happiness is the spiritual experience of living every minute with love, grace, and gratitude.

Dennis Waitley

At times our own light goes out and is rekindled by a spark from another person. Each of us has cause to think with deep gratitude of those who have lighted the flame within us.

Albert Schweitzer

You say grace before meals. All right. But I say grace before the concert and the opera, and grace before the play and pantomime, and grace before I open a book, and grace before sketching, painting, swimming, fencing, boxing, walking, playing, dancing and grace before I dip the pen in the ink.

G. K. Chesterton

*No duty is more urgent than that
of returning thanks.*

Unknown

*You simply will not be the same person two
months from now after consciously giving
thanks each day for the abundance that exists
in your life. And you will have set in motion
an ancient spiritual law: the more you have
and are grateful for, the more will be given you.*

Sarah Ban Breathnach

*Some people have a wonderful capacity
to appreciate again and again, freshly
and naively, the basic goods of life, with
awe, pleasure, wonder, and even ecstasy.*

Abraham Maslow

*We often take for granted the very things
that most deserve our gratitude.*

Cynthia Ozick

*Can you see the holiness in those things you
take for granted a paved road or a washing
machine? If you concentrate on finding what
is good in every situation, you will discover
that your life will suddenly be filled with
gratitude, a feeling that nurtures the soul.*

Rabbi Harold Kushner

When we become more fully aware that
our success is due in large measure to the
loyalty, helpfulness, and encouragement
we have received from others, our desire grows
to pass on similar gifts. Gratitude spurs us on
to prove ourselves worthy of what others
have done for us. The spirit of gratitude
is a powerful energizer.

Wilferd A. Peterson

Whatever our individual troubles and challenges
may be, it's important to pause every now and
then to appreciate all that we have, on every level.
We need to literally "count our blessings,"
give thanks for them, allow ourselves
to enjoy them, and relish the
experience of prosperity we already have.

Shakti Gawain

Thou that has given so much to me,
Give one thing more—a grateful heart;
Not thankful when it pleaseth me,
As if thy blessings had spare days;
But such a heart, whose pulse may be
Thy praise.

George Herbert

Find the good and praise it.

Alex Haley

Give thanks for a little and you will find a lot.

The Hausa of Nigeria

What if you gave someone a gift, and they neglected to thank you for it-would you be likely to give them another? Life is the same way. In order to attract more of the blessings that life has to offer, you must truly appreciate what you already have.

Ralph Marston

The moment one gives close attention to anything, even a blade of grass, it becomes a mysterious, awesome, indescribably magnificent world in itself.

Henry Miller

There is a calmness to a life lived in gratitude, a quiet joy.

Ralph H. Blum

Gratefulness is the key to a happy life that we hold in our hands, because if we are not grateful, then no matter how much we have we will not be happy — because we will always want to have something else or something more.

Brother David Steindl-Rast

As each day comes to us refreshed and anew, so does my gratitude renew itself daily. The breaking of the sun over the horizon

*is my grateful heart dawning upon
a blessed world.*

Adabella Radici

*For each new morning with its light,
For rest and shelter of the night,
For health and food, for love and friends,
For everything Thy goodness sends.*

Ralph Waldo Emerson

*Grace isn't a little prayer you chant before
receiving a meal. It's a way to live.*

Jacqueline Winspear

*When eating bamboo sprouts, remember
the man who planted them.*

Chinese Proverb

*But the value of gratitude does not consist solely in
getting you more blessings in the future. Without
gratitude you cannot long keep from dissatisfied
thought regarding things as they are.*

Wallace Wattles

*Blessed are those that can give without
remembering and receive without forgetting.*

Author Unknown

*Gratitude is a vaccine, an antitoxin,
and an antiseptic.*

John Henry Jowett

*Feeling grateful or appreciative of
someone or something in your life
actually attracts more of the things that
you appreciate and value into your life.*

Christiane Northrup

*The best way to pay for a lovely
moment is to enjoy it.*

Richard Bach

*Whenever we are appreciative, we are
filled with a sense of well-being and
swept up by the feeling of joy.*

M.J. Ryan

Gratitude is riches. Complaint is poverty.

Doris Day

*There is a law of gratitude, and it is . . . the
natural principle that action and reaction are
always equal and in opposite directions. The grateful
outreaching of your mind in thankful praise to
supreme intelligence is a liberation or expenditure
of force. It cannot fail to reach that to which it is*

addressed, and the reaction is an instantaneous movement toward you.

Wallace Wattles

Gratitude should not be just a reaction to getting what you want, but an all-the-time gratitude, the kind where you notice the little things and where you constantly look for the good, even in unpleasant situations. Start bringing gratitude to your experiences, instead of waiting for a positive experience in order to feel grateful.

Marelisa Fábrega

Let us rise up and be thankful, for if we didn't learn a lot today, at least we learned a little, and if we didn't learn a little, at least we didn't get sick, and if we got sick, at least we didn't die; so, let us all be thankful.

Buddha

Two kinds of gratitude: The sudden kind we feel for what we take; the larger kind we feel for what we give.

Edwin Arlington Robinson

Action For Happiness

After I had finished the first rough draft of this book, my Mother coincidentally sent me a newspaper cutting about a new movement called Action for Happiness that launched in April 2011.I was delighted to see how much it resonated with the content of the book and contacted Director Mark Williams to find out more about it. I am now an active and enthusiastic supporter of Action For happiness and would urge everyone to get involved in this brilliant initiative.

The Starfish Story at the end of part one of this book is a great example of how we can all make a difference .You can go on line today and make your pledge to help support and play a part in creating a happier society for everyone.

Here is some information about Action For happiness

Building a happier society together

Over the last 60 years we've seen huge material progress and unprecedented economic growth. Yet in terms of happiness we're still "stuck in the 50s". with surveys of life satisfaction showing that we're no happier now than we were then, despite all our apparent progress.

Although the material circumstances of our lives have improved, other trends have taken us in the wrong direction, causing more unhappiness. For example, we've seen increases in levels of anxiety and depression, more broken families, higher levels of inequality and lower levels of trust.

Action for Happiness is a movement of people committed to building a happier society. We want to see a fundamentally different way of life where people care less about what they can get for themselves and more about the happiness of others.

Our movement is bringing together like-minded people from all walks of life. It draws on the latest scientific research relating to happiness and is backed by leading experts from the fields of psychology, education, economics, social innovation and beyond.

Members of the movement make a simple pledge: to *"try to create more happiness and less unhappiness in the world around them"* through the way they approach their lives. We provide practical ideas to enable people to take action in different areas of their lives - at home, at work or in the community.

We launched in April 2011 and within three months had signed up around 15,000 members from over 100 different countries. Our first member was the Dalai Lama and others include high profile authors, philosophers and musicians as well as leading figures from the worlds of business, sport and the arts. We have no religious, political or commercial affiliations and we welcome people of all faiths (or none), political backgrounds and parts of society.

Our vision is of a happier society, where as many people as possible are living happy, fulfilling lives and as few people as possible are leading unhappy lives. This vision includes:

✓ Families that are loving, stable and well equipped to raise happy children
✓ An education system which equips children with capabilities needed to live happy lives
✓ People giving time and energy to be actively involved in their communities
✓ Employers creating positive working environments and having happy staff
✓ A healthier society with less mental illness and addiction
✓ Balanced lifestyles, allowing quality time with families, friends and communities
✓ Higher levels of trust and equality
✓ People finding inner peace and contentment
✓ Government policy realigned to measure and prioritise wellbeing.

Our mission is to inspire and enable the move to a happier society, by promoting the latest research on happiness, inspiring people to join the movement and enabling them to take positive action in their personal lives, homes, schools, workplaces and communities. We are also pushing for a much greater focus on happiness and well-being in public policy.

Visit www.actionforhappiness.org for more information.

Reference and Recommended Reading

Thanks: How the New Science of Gratitude Can Make You Happier - Robert Emmons

The Happiness Purpose: Edward De Bono

Motivate to Win - Richard Denny

Wellbeing - Cary Cooper and Ivan Robertson

Authentic Happiness: Using the New Positive Psychology to Realise Your Potential for Lasting Fulfilment - Martin Seligman

Learning to Think Strategically - Julia Stone

Meditation - The Stress Solution - Mary Pearson

Mind Power - James Borg

What's the Point? A Guide to Life and Happiness - Anthony Peters

Authentic: How to Make a Living by Being Yourself - Neil Crofts

Brilliant Cognitive Behavioural Therapy: How to Use CBT to Improve Your Mind and Your Life - Dr Stephen Briers

Change your life with CBT - Corinne Sweet

Change Your Thinking - Change Your Life - Brian Tracy

Character Strengths and Virtues: A Handbook and Classification - Christopher Peterson and Martin Seligman

Flow: The Psychology of Happiness: The Classic Work on How to Achieve Happiness - Mihaly Csikszentmihalyi

Happiness - Richard Layard

How to Make Yourself Happy and Remarkably Less Disturbable - Albert Ellis

Happier - Tal Ben-Shahar

Learned Optimism - Martin Seligman

Positive Psychology for Dummies - Averil Leimon & Gladeana McMahon

Reinventing the Sacred - Stuart Kaufman

The A – Z of Good Mental Health - Jeremy Thomas and Dr Tony Hughes

The American Paradox: Spiritual Hunger in an Age of Plenty - Dr David G. Myers, author of

The Big Society - Jesse Norman

The Constitution of Society: Outline of the Theory of Structuration - Anthony Giddens

The Happiness Hypothesis: Putting Ancient Wisdom to the Test of Modern Science -Jonathan Haidt

The Life You Were Born to Live - Dan Millman

The Practice of Rational Emotive Behavior Therapy - Albert Ellis

A Primer in Positive Psychology - Christopher Peterson

About the Author

Liggy Webb is based in the UK and is widely respected as a leading expert in the field of Modern Life Skills. As a presenter, consultant and author she is passionate about her work and improving the quality of people's lives. She has developed a range of techniques and strategies to support individuals and organisations to cope more effectively and successfully with modern living and the demands and challenges of life in the twenty tens and beyond.

Visit www.liggywebb.com for more information.

Motivational Presentations

Liggy is noted for her dynamic and engaging style and as a result is frequently invited to present and speak at international conferences, award ceremonies, on board cruise ships, in the media and at a variety of high profile events.

Her experience and expertise is a blend of behavioural change, holistic health and positive psychology.

Contact info@liggywebb.com for more information on presentations.

Books & Publications

Author of *The Happy Handbook - A Compendium of Modern Life Skills*

Author of *How to Work Wonders - Your Guide to Workplace Wellness*

Contributing author of *The Business Leaders Club - Lessons Learned from the Recession.*

Executive Editor for *Training Pages* - www.training ages.com

Author of Workplace Wellness paper *People Alchemy* - www.peoplealchemy.co.uk.

Monthly column in The Cheltonian - www.thecheltonian.co.uk.

Liggy is the founder of The Montpellier Writing group www.montpellierwriters.co.nr in October 2007

Liggy's next book is out in 2012 for more information email info@liggywebb.com

Consultancy

Liggy is a consultant for the United Nations and travels extensively working in a variety of worldwide locations. She is also the founding director of The Learning Architect, an international learning and development organisation.

Visit www.thelearningarchitect.com

Charity

Liggy is a trustee of The Chrysalis Foundation www.chrysalisprogramme.com and actively supports mental health charities as well Action For Happiness www.actionforhappiness.org

Purpose

Liggy is passionate about supporting people with depression and helping people to live more positive lives.

Free Materials

For free downloadable toolkits and articles visit www.liggywebb.com

Acknowledgements

There are many people who have been instrumental in helping me to make this book happen and I would like to thank everyone who has been involved .I would also like to make a special acknowledgement to the following people who have made an extra special contribution.

I owe so much of the content of this book to my Mother and Father ,two amazing people who have given me so much love, support, laughter and inspiration.

Kate Tuck and Lawrence Mclhoney - Because I really couldn't get any of this off the ground without you.

Andy Veitch, Sara Pankhurst ,Melanie Lisney, Jacky Leonard, Lois Grant, Isobel Sherrington, Francis Sherrington, Paula Evans, Jacky Pearson, Charles Christie - Webb, Aubrey Stuart.

Everyone who is part of The Learning Architect.

The rich tapestry of talent that is the Montpellier Writing Group

All my colleagues at the UN - I feel privileged to be part of the team.

Special thanks for the wisdom that has shaped my thinking - Edward De Bono, Richard Denny and Paul O'Neill.

And to all my friends who are the charming gardeners who make my soul blossom.

Thank You

158

28 Day Gratitude Journal

Day One

Today's Highlights

1. ....

2. ....

3. ....

I am grateful for

....

....

....

....

....

....

....

....

....

....

....

....

....

....

....

....

....

....

....

....

....

....

....

....

Day Two

Today's Highlights

1. ....

2. ....

3. ....

I am grateful for

....

....

....

....

....

....

....

....

....

....

....

....
....
....
....
....
....
....
....
....
....
....
....
....
....
....
....
....
....

Day Three

Today's Highlights

1. ....

2. ....

3. ....

I am grateful for

....

....

....

....

....

....

....

....

....

....

....

....

....

....

....

....

....

....

....

....

....

....

....

....

....

....

....

....

Day Four

Today's Highlights

1. ....

2. ....

3. ....

I am grateful for

....

....

....

....

....

....

....

....

....

....

....

....

....

....

....

....

....

....

....

....

....

....

....

....

....

....

....

....

Day Five

Today's Highlights

1. ....

2. ....

3. ....

I am grateful for

....

....

....

....

....

....

....

....

....

....

....

....

....

....

....

....

....

....

....

....

....

....

....

....

....

....

....

....

Day Six

Today's Highlights

1. ....

2. ....

3. ....

I am grateful for

....

....

....

....

....

....

....

....

....

....

....

....

....

....

....

....

....

....

....

....

....

....

....

....

....

....

....

....

....

Day Seven

Today's Highlights

1. ....

2. ....

3. ....

I am grateful for

....

....

....

....

....

....

....

....

....

....

....

....

....

....

....

....

....

....

....

....

....

....

....

....

....

....

....

....

....

Day Eight

Today's Highlights

1. ....

2. ....

3. ....

I am grateful for

....

....

....

....

....

....

....

....

....

....

....

....
....
....
....
....
....
....
....
....
....
....
....
....
....
....
....
....

Day Nine

Today's Highlights

1. ....

2. ....

3. ....

I am grateful for

....

....

....

....

....

....

....

....

....

....

....

....

....

....

....

....

....

....

....

....

....

....

....

....

....

....

....

Day Ten

Today's Highlights

1. ....

2. ....

3. ....

I am grateful for

....

....

....

....

....

....

....

....

....

....

....

....

....

....

....

....

....

....

....

....

....

....

....

....

....

....

....

Day Eleven

Today's Highlights

1. ....

2. ....

3. ....

I am grateful for

....

....

....

....

....

....

....

....

....

....

....

....

....

....

....

....

....

....

....

....

....

....

....

....

....

....

....

Day Twelve

Today's Highlights

1. ....

2. ....

3. ....

I am grateful for

....

....

....

....

....

....

....

....

....

....

....

....

....

....

....

....

....

....

....

....

....

....

....

....

....

....

....

Day Thirteen

Today's Highlights

1. ....

2. ....

3. ....

I am grateful for

....

....

....

....

....

....

....

....

....

....

....

....
....
....
....
....
....
....
....
....
....
....
....
....
....
....
....
....
....

Day Fourteen

Today's Highlights

1. ....

2. ....

3. ....

I am grateful for

....

....

....

....

....

....

....

....

....

....

....

....

....

....

....

....

....

....

....

....

....

....

....

....

....

....

....

....

Day Fifteen

Today's Highlights

1. ....

2. ....

3. ....

I am grateful for

....

....

....

....

....

....

....

....

....

....

....

....

....

....

....

....

....

....

....

....

....

....

....

....

....

....

....

....

....

Day Sixteen

Today's Highlights

1. ....

2. ....

3. ....

I am grateful for

....

....

....

....

....

....

....

....

....

....

....

....

....

....

....

....

....

....

....

....

....

....

....

....

....

....

....

Day Seventeen

Today's Highlights

1. ....

2. ....

3. ....

I am grateful for

....

....

....

....

....

....

....

....

....

....

....

....

....

....

....

....

....

....

....

....

....

....

....

....

....

....

....

....

Day Eighteen

Today's Highlights

1. ....

2. ....

3. ....

I am grateful for

....

....

....

....

....

....

....

....

....

....

....

....

....

....

....

....

....

....

....

....

....

....

....

....

....

....

....

....

Day Nineteen

Today's Highlights

1. ....

2. ....

3. ....

I am grateful for

....

....

....

....

....

....

....

....

....

....

....
....
....
....
....
....
....
....
....
....
....
....
....
....
....
....
....

Day Twenty

Today's Highlights

1. ....

2. ....

3. ....

I am grateful for

....

....

....

....

....

....

....

....

....

....

....

....

....

....

....

....

....

....

....

....

....

....

....

....

....

....

....

....

....

Day Twenty-one

Today's Highlights

1. ....

2. ....

3. ....

I am grateful for

....

....

....

....

....

....

....

....

....

....

....

....
....
....
....
....
....
....
....
....
....
....
....
....
....
....
....
....
....

Day Twenty-two

Today's Highlights

1. ....

2. ....

3. ....

I am grateful for

....

....

....

....

....

....

....

....

....

....

....

....
....
....
....
....
....
....
....
....
....
....
....
....
....
....
....
....

Day Twenty-three

Today's Highlights

1. ....

2. ....

3. ....

I am grateful for

....

....

....

....

....

....

....

....

....

....

....

....

....

....

....

....

....

....

....

....

....

....

....

....

....

....

....

....

Day Twenty-four

Today's Highlights

1. ....

2. ....

3. ....

I am grateful for

....

....

....

....

....

....

....

....

....

....

....

....

....

....

....

....

....

....

....

....

....

....

....

....

....

....

....

....

Day Twenty-five

Today's Highlights

1. ....

2. ....

3. ....

I am grateful for

....

....

....

....

....

....

....

....

....

....

....

....
....
....
....
....
....
....
....
....
....
....
....
....
....
....
....
....
....

Day Twenty-six

Today's Highlights

1. ....

2. ....

3. ....

I am grateful for

....

....

....

....

....

....

....

....

....

....

....

....

....

....

....

....

....

....

....

....

....

....

....

....

....

....

....

....

Day Twenty-seven

Today's Highlights

1. ....

2. ....

3. ....

I am grateful for

....

....

....

....

....

....

....

....

....

....

....

....

....

....

....

....

....

....

....

....

....

....

....

....

....

....

....

....

Day Twenty-eight

Today's Highlights

1. ....

2. ....

3. ....

I am grateful for

....

....

....

....

....

....

....

....

....

....

....

....

....

....

....

....

....

....

....

....

....

....

....

....

....

....

....

Lightning Source UK Ltd.
Milton Keynes UK
UKOW051411260112

186130UK00001B/38/P